UNITED STATES CRYPTOLOGIC HISTORY

Series IV

World War II

Volume 7

The Quiet Heroes of the Southwest Pacific Theater: An Oral History of the Men and Women of CBB and FRUMEL

Sharon A. Maneki

CENTER FOR CRYPTOLOGIC HISTORY

NATIONAL SECURITY AGENCY

Reprinted 2007

This monograph is a product of the National Security Agency history program. Its contents and conclusions are those of the author, based on original research, and do not necessarily represent the official views of the National Security Agency. Please address divergent opinion or additional detail to the Center for Cryptologic History (EC).

Table of Contents

Foreword

The Central Bureau Brisbane (CBB) and the Fleet Radio Unit Melbourne (FRUMEL) played vital, if largely unheralded, parts in supporting military operations in the Southwest Pacific in World War ll. The communications intelligence (COMINT) they produced was often a major factor in decision making by General Douglas MacArthur, his staff, and other senior leaders in the struggle to prevent further Japanese conquests and to retake captured territory.

The Quiet Heroes of the Southwest Pacific Theater: An Oral History of the Men and Women of CBB and FRUMEL by Ms. Sharon Maneki of the Center for Cryptologic History fills many gaps in our knowledge of CBB and FRUMEL. It is an important book because Ms. Maneki has presented a unique portrait of the COMINT production process in wartime.

COMINT production in World War II was an extremely complex endeavor. One major theme of *The Quiet Heroes of the Southwest Pacific Theater* is how diverse aspects of the process combined to produce the intelligence distributed to commanders. Of particular interest is the subtle and supportive interplay between cryptanalysis and traffic analysis. Other factors, such as rudimentary machine processing and lucky discoveries on the battlefield, also contributed to the process.

As a complex and cooperative process, however, the production of COMINT depended on a strong organizational structure which could meld components and make them work – and work quickly enough to produce COMINT in time for operational use. It is not a contradiction to say that this organization also needed a structure which would get the best out of its brilliant staff. CBB and FRUMEL were successful in both counts.

The Quiet Heroes of the Southwest Pacific Theater is highly recommended; it should have a place on the bookshelf of every scholar interested in the Pacific War or the professional study of communications intelligence.

David A. Hatch
NSA Historian
Center for Cryptologic History

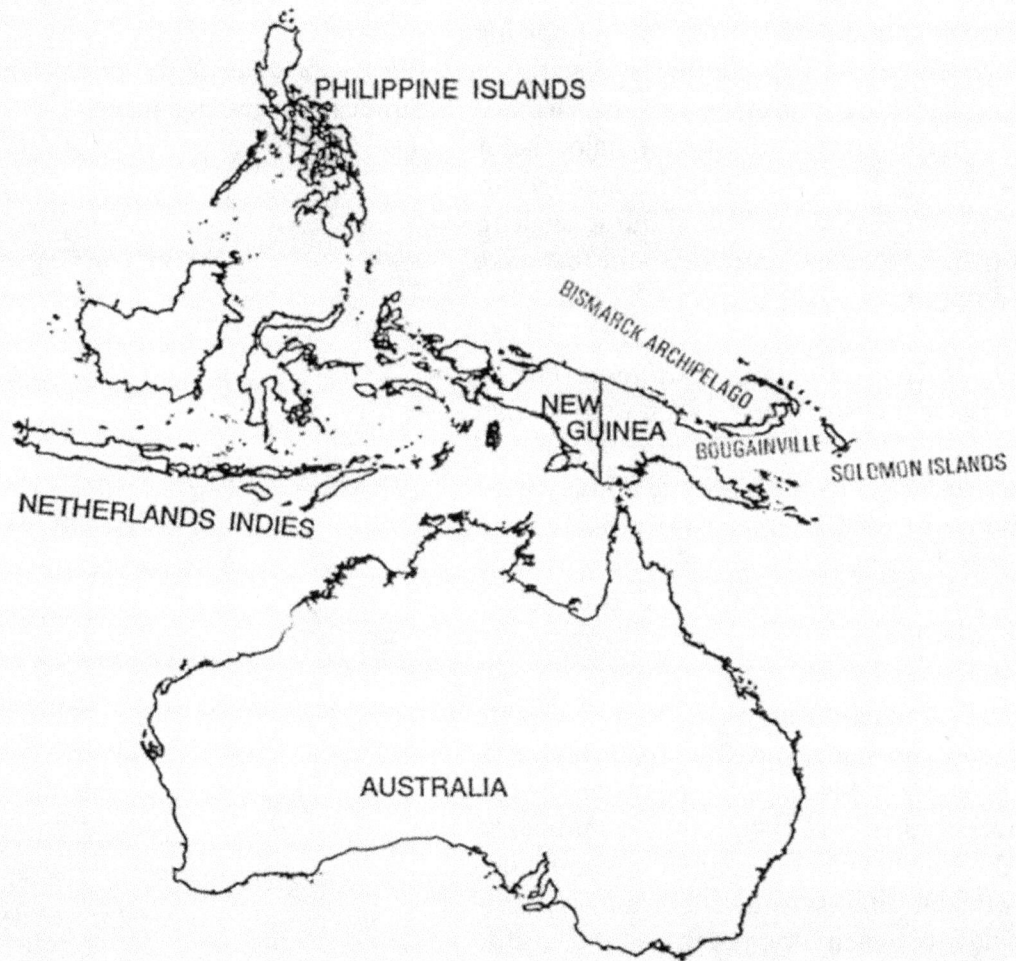

The Southwest Pacific theater, MacArthur's domain of responsibility during WWII, presented unique challenges because of the distances.

Preface

In World War II, the Japanese were a bold, formidable enemy for the Allies. The Southwest Pacific theater covered an immense area: it included Australia, New Guinea, the Northern Solomon Islands, the Bismarck Archipelago, and the Philippines. Allied commander General Douglas MacArthur's objectives were to stop the advancing Japanese, to return to the Philippines, and, eventually, to invade Japan itself. Communications intelligence was a great asset to MacArthur in meeting these objectives. The war In the Pacific was shortened by at least two years because of the efforts of the communications intelligence practitioners who produced ULTRA, information derived from reading the Japanese military codes. What were some of ULTRA's accomplishments in the Southwest Pacific theater?

ULTRA provided Allied commanders with an astonishing range of data about the Japanese army, air force, and navy. ULTRA immeasurably simplified the interdiction of air and sea resupply routes because it foretold the locations and times that Japanese ships and aircraft would appear. General George C. Kenny, MacArthur's air corps commander, began with small attacks against Japanese convoys at Buna, New Guinea, but quickly moved to orchestrate the battle of the Bismarck Sea. The near annihilation of the Japanese army's Fifty-first Division at sea marked the strategic turning point of the New Guinea operation, which enabled MacArthur's 1943 ground campaign to move forward. Kenny's destruction of Japanese aircraft at Wewak in August 1943 made possible MacArthur's invasion of Lae, New Guinea, and his war of attrition at Rabaul made possible the invasion of the Admiralties. Kenny's destruction of Japanese air power at Hollandia during March and April 1944 made possible MacArthur's greatest leapfrog operation along the northern New Guinea coast. In late 1944, ULTRA allowed Kenny's airmen to exact a terrible price on Japanese ships and men going to Leyte. The interdiction campaign not only thwarted Japanese attempts to bolster their defenses in the Southwest Pacific but also forced them to abandon large garrisons that could no longer be resupplied.

The Allies' ability to read Japanese army messages definitely shortened the ground war in the Pacific. ULTRA identified the operational flaw in MacArthur's New Guinea campaign by exposing Japanese intentions to vigorously defend Hansa Bay. Instead, MacArthur bypassed Hansa Bay and struck deep behind enemy lines at Hollandia. ULTRA also played a major role in the timing and planning of this campaign. On 22 April 1944, Allied aircraft simultaneously attacked Hollandia, Aitape, and Wakde-Sarmi. ULTRA's greatest contribution to MacArthur's strategy was in this Hollandia campaign. One of the most important intelligence coups that came from reading the Japanese Army Water Transport Code was the discovery of the *Take* convoy. In late April and early May 1944, U.S. submarines sank this convoy, causing the Japanese to lose all of their equipment and approximately 3,954 troops. The Japanese plan to reinforce their defenses in western New Guinea with the Thirty-second and Thirty-fifth Divisions was foiled. The *Take* disaster allowed MacArthur to speed up the invasion of Wakde and Biak and made his victories in western New Guinea possible. Consequently, MacArthur was also able to advance his timetable for reaching the Philippines. ULTRA and those who produced it saved lives and shortened the war in the Pacific. ULTRA is one of the great intellectual, technological, and military triumphs of World War II.

In today's push-button society, where opportunities for instant information and instant gratification abound, it is difficult to appreciate the amount

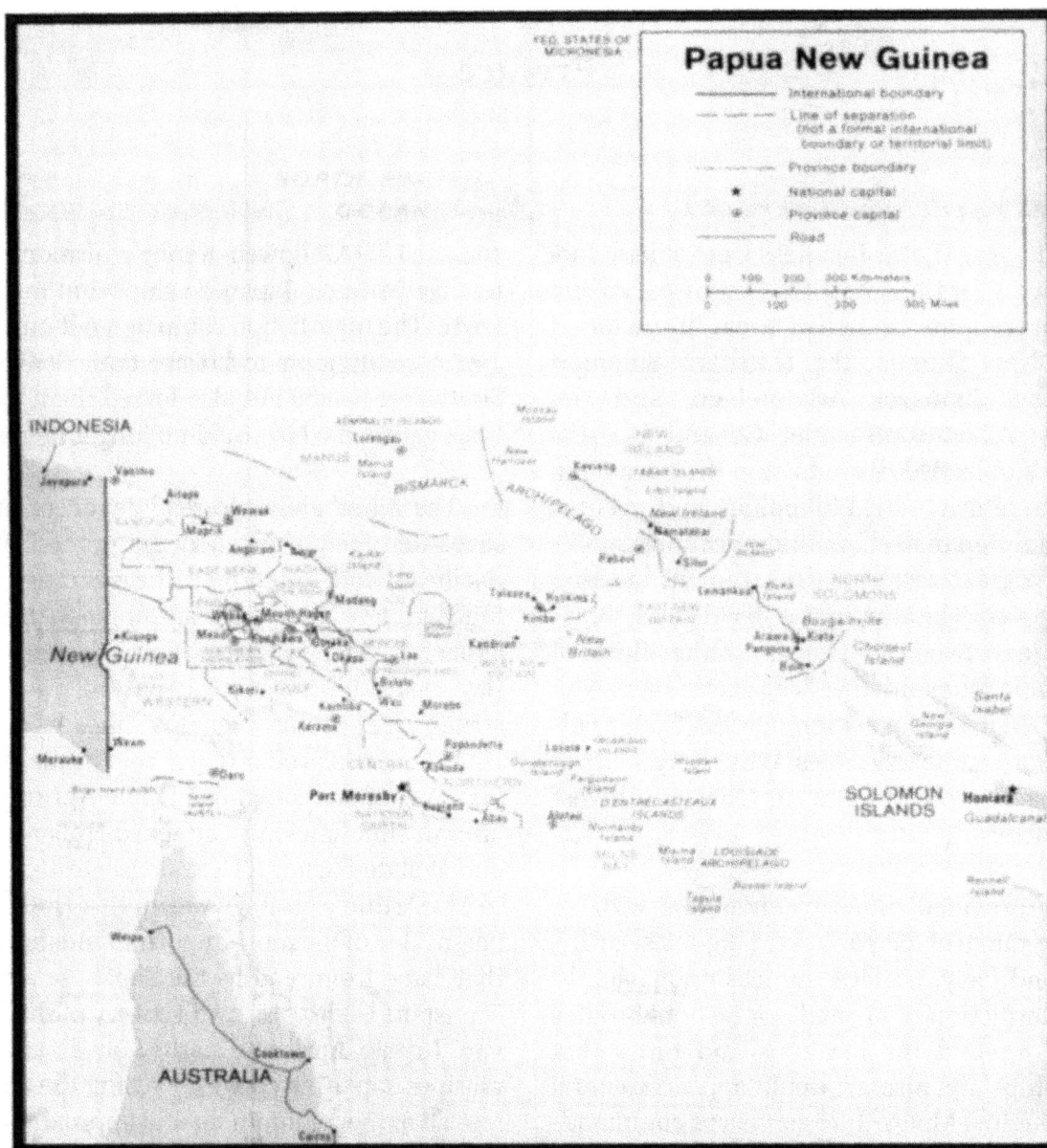

MacArthur's island hopping campaign through New Guinea in 1943 and 1944 was a stepping stone to his objective to return to the Philippines.

of research, study, analysis, and grueling work involved in exploiting information from enemy codes during World War II. Historians appropriately applaud the achievements of breaking the codes but have little understanding of the herculean team efforts that were put forth to break the codes, keep up with changes in the codes, exploit the intelligence, and get it to the people who needed it.

Some historians incorrectly credit the successful reading of codes only to the cryptanalysts. The Central Bureau Brisbane and Fleet Radio Unit Melbourne experiences demonstrated the interdependence of collection, traffic analysis, and cryptanalysis. Central Bureau had little success in 1942 because it took time to get intercept units established. Traffic analysts and cryptanalysts need sufficient amounts of material for research and study. The cryptanalyst depends on the traffic analyst to identify message centers and addresses. By associating locations with broadcasts of particular military units, the traffic analyst inferred troop deployments and forthcoming operations. Traffic analysis activities were the first step in compiling an accu-

Jayapura, formerly Hollandia, was MacArthur's greatest leap forward in the New Guinea campaign.

rate Japanese order of battle. There were many instances during the war when traffic analysis was MacArthur's major or only source of signals intelligence because codes were unreadable at the time. One instance was the Japanese attack on Port Moresby, New Guinea, in July 1942. Another time traffic analysis had to fill the void was when the Japanese army changed their codes on 8 April 1944, as MacArthur was planning the Hollandia invasion, which was to begin on 22 April 1944.

Cryptanalysis was also a source of assistance to the traffic analyst. In New Guinea, some Japanese air bases were so close together that they could be identified only by reading designations in the army codes.

This is an oral history of the activities outlining all of the varied tasks involved in code breaking. This is the story of participants from all sectors of the communications intelligence operation in the Southwest Pacific theater. Success would have been impossible without sustained effort on tedious tasks such as recording message numbers, filing messages by callsign or code group, keypunching IBM cards, and copying and subtracting numbers to find the pattern in code groups, day after day, year after year throughout the war.

Success depended on intercept operators who had to copy Kana with accuracy and speed. Copying Kana is frustrating because it is a code of seventy-one symbols rather than the twenty-six-letter international code. Success depended on translators who struggled to interpret the complexities of the Japanese language. There are numerous stories of individuals who came back on their own time to work on the solution of a problem or to catch up with an ever-increasing work load. Their persistence and dedication were remarkable.

It is appropriate for this oral history to contain the recollections of people from all sectors of communications intelligence. This monograph not only contains recollections from intercept operators, traffic analysts, cryptanalysts, and linguists connected with Central Bureau and the Fleet Radio Unit Melbourne but also covers these disciplines from different perspectives. These perspectives include officers versus enlisted men, Americans versus Australians, and the role of women in communications intelligence. Much of the monograph is devoted to experiences at Central Bureau because it was a larger organization than the Fleet Radio Unit Melbourne and, thus, more sources were available. These interviews were conducted by oral historians at the Center for Cryptologic History in the National Security Agency. The production of this monograph would have been impossible without the research and interviewing skills of Robert Farley. Mr. Farley located and interviewed 90 percent of the subjects in this collection. He recognized the importance of their story.

Robert Farley

As is true of any oral history, memories fade, and there is sometimes inconsistency in some details such as dates. However, the interviews give an accurate picture of what life was like in the Southwest Pacific theater for these quiet heroes. They give us an appreciation of the tremendous challenges they faced. The production of communications intelligence was truly a team effort.

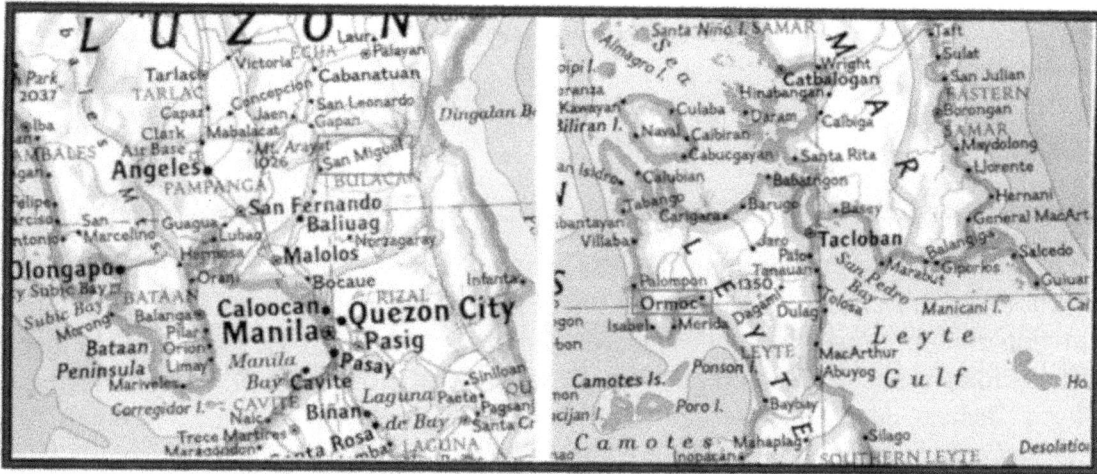

As the war front moved to the Philippines in 1945, Central Bureau set up its headquarters in San Miguel, Luzon.

The discovery of the Japanese resupply convoy in Ormoc Bay was an important SIGINT achievement.

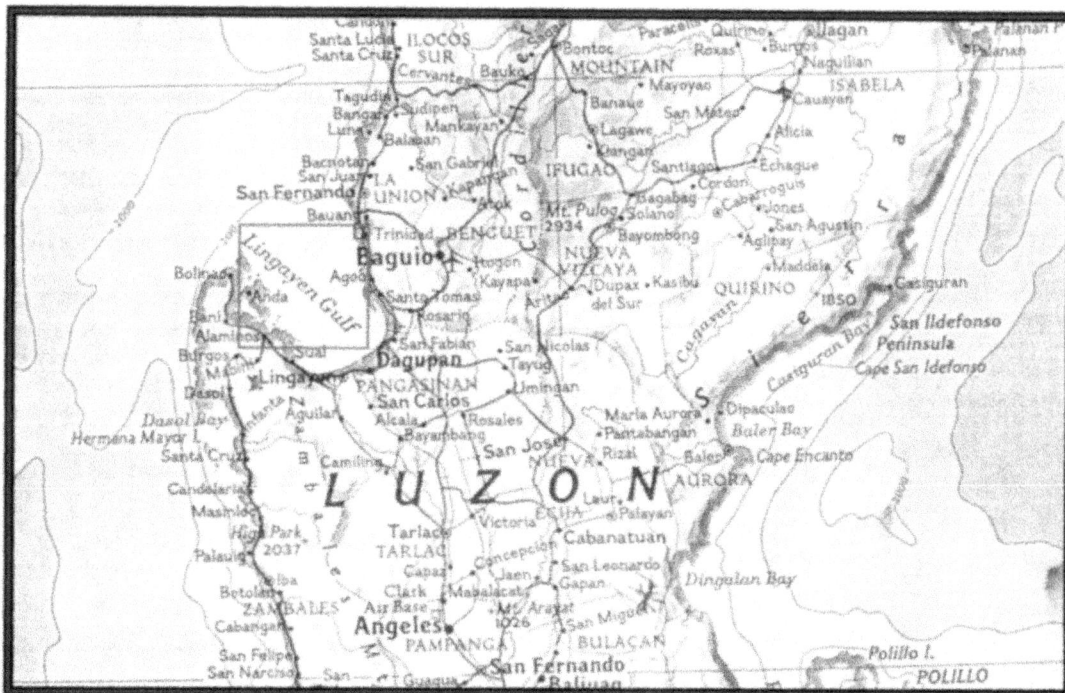

The Allies entered Lingayen Gulf on 9 January 1945.

Acknowledgments

I wish to express my appreciation to the following individuals for their invaluable contributions to the production of this publication: the staff of the NSA Geographic Library for their assistance in the collection and production of maps; my colleagues at the Center for Cryptologic History, Dr. Tom Johnson and Beverly Warren, for guidance in the research and initial editing of the manuscript; the publications team of the Center, Barry Carleen, Jean Persinger, and Laura Clark, for their superb efforts in completing the design layout and final editing of the project. Lu Greenwood of the publications team also made outstanding contributions to the reformatting and reprinting of the monograph.

Sharon Maneki

An Introduction to the Central Bureau Story

General Douglas MacArthur established the Central Bureau (later referred to as CBB) on 15 April 1942. Central Bureau's overall mission was to obtain intelligence from Japanese military signals, protect the security of Allied communications, work with Arlington Hall in Washington, D.C., to solve Japanese military (especially army) cryptographic codes, and to support the U.S. Navy and British commands in nearby theaters as appropriate. The nearby theaters supported by Central Bureau were the Central Pacific, South Pacific, and the China-Burma-India (CBI) theater areas.

Central Bureau was a joint organization made up of the U.S. Army, Australian Imperial Forces (AIF), and the Royal Australian Air Force (RAAF). MacArthur's chief signals officer, Major General Spencer B. Akin, was the director of Central Bureau. A joint committee of each of the three services determined Central Bureau policy. In 1942, the commanding officers who sat on this policy committee were Colonel Joseph Scherr, USA; Captain A. W. Sandford, AIF; and Flight Lieutenant H. R. Booth, RAAF. After the death of Colonel Scherr in 1943, Colonel Abraham Sinkov sat on this joint committee for the remainder of the war. Colonel Sinkov was responsible for much of the success of Central Bureau.

Although there were many Allied joint military organizations in World War II, few can match the harmony and cooperation found in Central Bureau. This was a remarkable achievement because its workforce consisted of representatives from fourteen services and many nationalities including American, Australian, British, Canadian, New Zealander, French, and Filipino. Central Bureau needed highly skilled personnel and recruited them from any source possible.

Major Geoffrey Ballard, an AIF officer assigned to Central Bureau, offers an interesting explanation for this high level of cooperation. He points out how bleak things looked for the Allies in the Pacific in 1942. Ballard relates that after the Japanese attack on Pearl Harbor, the Australians feared they would be next. Prior to 1942, Australian troops were helping the British on various war fronts. In January 1942, expecting a Japanese invasion, the Australian government ordered all of its troops to return home to protect the homeland. Australia was definitely anxious for U.S. help.

A second reason for the high level of cooperation within Central Bureau offered by Colonel Charles E. Girhard, a U.S. Army officer who established the cryptologic section at Central Bureau, was the clear division of labor between the Americans and the Australians. Girhard points out that the Americans were responsible for cryptanalytic tasks, and the Australians were responsible for traffic analytic tasks. This division of labor was based on expertise. The Australians had little cryptanalytic experience. However, Australia had troops who acquired traffic analysis experience while serving with the British in Africa and the Middle East. By the end of the war, Central Bureau had 4,339 personnel, including its field sections.

From its inception, MacArthur intended that as a support organization, Central Bureau should be close to his general headquarters. When MacArthur's general headquarters moved from Melbourne to Brisbane in July 1942, CBB moved there in September 1942. When MacArthur's general headquarters moved to Hollandia in August 1944, an echelon of CBB followed in November. When MacArthur moved to Manila in March 1945, CBB moved almost its entire operation to San Miguel over the period from May to July 1945. By the end of the war, the scope of CBB activities covered an area from Okinawa in the north to Brisbane in the south, as far west as Guam and as far east as Borneo. The achievements of CBB participants are especially remarkable in light of the distance, geographic conditions, and logistical problems they had to contend with.

Brisbane, capital city of Queensland

Stony Bridge

Brisbane area (photo not identified)

Downtown Queen Street featured shops, banks, restaurants, and modern theatres.

Chapter 1
The Challenge of Reaching Australia

Early 1942 was a bleak period for the Allies in the Southwest Pacific theater. The Japanese conquest of Pacific territory proceeded with alarming speed. By the end of March 1942, the Japanese controlled Hong Kong, Rangoon, Singapore, the Philippines, and the Dutch East Indies. General MacArthur was forced out of the Philippines and established his new headquarters in Melbourne, Australia, on 21 March 1942.

The Americans who worked in communications intelligence (COMINT) came to Australia either because they had to escape from the Philippines or because they were sent there from the U.S. by the Army. Each route had its challenges. Both the U.S. Army and the U.S. Navy had intercept units on Corregidor. Intercept units were especially important because of their skills and because of the information they could reveal to the Japanese if captured. The U.S. Navy, and later the Army, saw the prudence of getting these men out of Corregidor. Their escapes were no easy feats. The following accounts by Chief Radioman (later Captain) Duane L. Whitlock and Lieutenant (later Colonel) Howard W. Brown illustrate this point. Lieutenant (later Colonel) Charles Girhard came to Australia directly from the U.S. His account illustrates the problems the U.S. faced in gearing up for the war effort in the Pacific.

Escaping the Philippines: A View from the Navy

Duane Whitlock joined the Navy in 1935. After serving on a light cruiser as a radioman, he was selected for special intercept training at OP-20-G. He served at intercept sites in Hawaii and Guam. He came to the Philippines in July 1940 and was a member of the traffic analysis unit on Corregidor. As part of the third evacuation group, his twenty-day ordeal from Corregidor to Fremantle, Australia, which began on 16 March 1942, was certainly memorable.

My escape got off to an ominous start. My first surprise was that the submarine Permit was not waiting at the dock for the arrival of our group. We took launch boats out to look for the sub. We were able to chase the sub down because it had to stay on the surface until it cleared the mines. When we got on board, we found that we were not the only evacuees on the boat. The men who were evacuated from our unit earlier that day were also on board. The coast watchers did not realize that the Permit came back to port so they mistakenly set another evacuation

Duane Whitlock

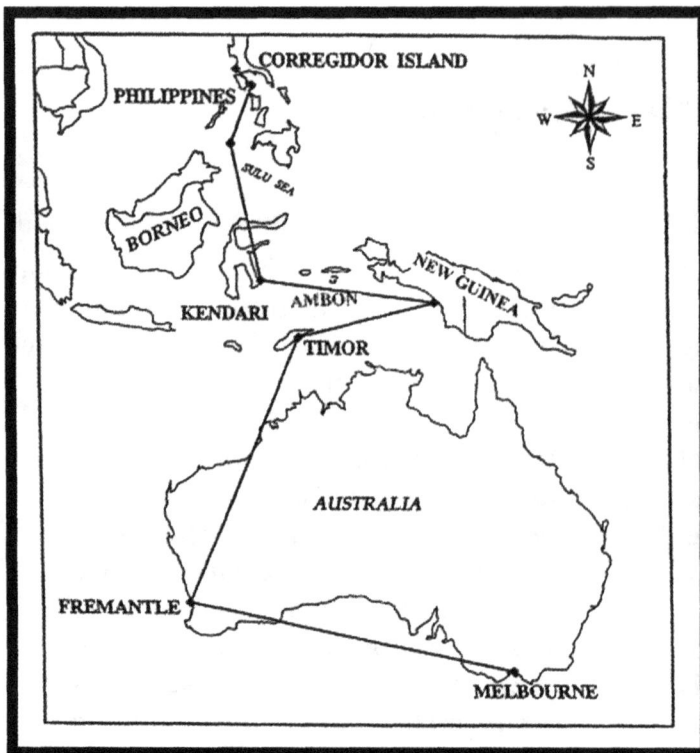

Duane Whitlock's escape route from Corregidor in March 1942

in motion because they thought a new submarine came in. As a result, this submarine, which normally holds 60 people, had 120 people on board. It was so overcrowded that if you were not on watch, you had to lay [sic] in your bunk since there was no place else to go.

Because of security and the 'need to know' principle, I began this voyage in a difficult predicament. The captain, Moon Chapel, had orders to break patrol and proceed to Australia immediately. This captain was a charger, so instead of breaking patrol and going to the open waters of the South China Sea, he headed through the Philippine Islands to the Sulu Sea. Through traffic analysis, I knew that there was a Japanese [division] of

destroyers off the islands south of Corregidor cleaning up interisland shipping. Did I have the authority to give Captain Chapel this information? Was the captain cleared to receive such information? After discussing this dilemma with others from my unit, we agreed that I did not have the authority to give this information to the captain. The next night, he surfaced right in the middle of the Japanese destroyers. We submerged, and the submarine was under depth charge attack for [twenty]-eight hours. The heat was unbearable because we had to turn off all the cooling systems. The temperature of the water was 83 degrees at induction and we were so overcrowded. Such a long submersion reduced our oxygen levels; there was so little oxygen that you could not even light a match. We finally escaped. I would not repeat that experience even for a million dollars.

A second close call came several days later when the submarine was between Kendari [Celebes, Indonesia], and Ambon. We spotted a Japanese merchant ship at extreme range heading south. We chased that ship all afternoon, but since it made the same speed as we did, we could not catch it. Shortly before dark, the captain decided to fire two torpedoes at this ship, which was about 7,000 yards away. Almost immediately after the torpedoes were touched off, I heard the order 'crash dive! crash dive!' One of the damn fish went out and circled around and came right back *at us! We went down about 155 feet, and [it] went right over the top of us. You could even hear the screws on the thing.*

Toward the end of the voyage, when the submarine was southeast of Timor, we had a third very close call. I was sitting in the dinette area surrounded by racks of dishes. I noticed that we were at a steep angle and the stern was dropping. The dishes began to spill out of their racks. Captain Chapel jumped out of his bunk and yelled: 'What the hell is going on here!' The captain discovered that one of the crew pumped the trim tanks inward instead of outward, sending water into the control room. By the time the captain caught this mistake, the water was within six inches of our electric motors. We were very lucky to get out of that one.

After landing at Fremantle, Whitlock and his companions went to Melbourne by train and joined the Fleet Radio Unit at Melbourne (FRUMEL). Whitlock served at FRUMEL until October 1943, when he returned to Washington, D.C., to serve at naval cryptologic headquarters. FRUMEL was established in February 1942 by merging U.S. signals intelligence (SIGINT) naval personnel from Corregidor under the command of Lieutenant Commander Rudolph J. Fabian with the small Australian naval SIGINT unit.

Escaping the Philippines: A View from the Army

Howard W. Brown joined the Army in the early 1930s. He was assigned to the Tenth Signal Service Company as a telegraph operator at Fort Santiago, Manila, in 1932. He became fascinated with the Japanese Kana code so he taught himself how to copy it. After attending radio electrician school at Fort Monmouth, New Jersey, he joined the Signals

Intelligence Detachment of the Fifty-first Battalion. He returned to the Philippines at the end of 1934 to do intercept activities. In the late 1930s, Brown took a job with the McKay radio station in Manila. In 1941, he was commissioned as a second lieutenant and served under Major (later Colonel) Joseph R. Scherr as the operations officer in an army intercept unit in the Philippines. Shortly after MacArthur left Corregidor, General Wainwright, the U.S. commander in the Philippines, received instructions to send Brown and ten other enlisted men to Australia. Brown's orders were to proceed to Del Monte on the northern coast of Mindanao, in the Philippines, establish an intercept station, and await further instructions. Brown's description of his 28 March 1942 escape in a B-17 follows:

We could see the lights of the city of Manila from Bataan Field, but as soon as we turned the field lights on so that the planes could take off, Manila was blacked out. We flew over Corregidor at about 3,000 feet and the searchlights caught us. The anti- aircraft command had been notified that we were going over, but we held our breath for several eternities, not

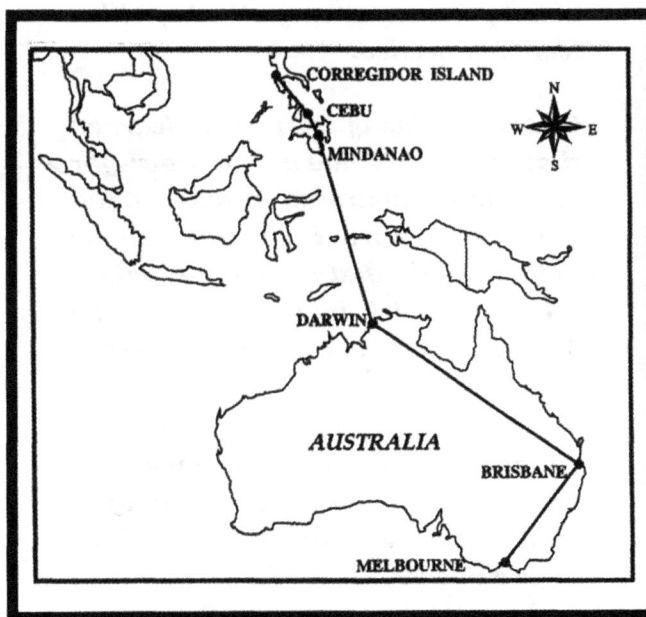

Howard Brown's escape route from Corregidor in April 1942

knowing when some trigger-happy illegitimate might open fire – because when one shoots, they all shoot. The lights went off, no shots – Whew!!

We landed at Cebu at daylight, camouflaged the planes in a cane field, and drove into town. Cebu [an island about 400 miles south of Manila] was a peaceful little place that had been attacked only twice – once by strafing planes and once by a destroyer that dropped a few shells into the business district. At about 1600 hours, we took off, skipped the water down to Del Monte, Mindanao, and landed just after dark.

We established an intercept unit of sorts between the airfield and a pineapple plantation by 'acquiring' four receivers, a diesel generator, and a wiring cutout of an old B-17 on the ground. Soon we were in business, monitoring Japanese aircraft movements, and passing on air raid warnings as well as our own hunches about potential enemy attacks, which were not heeded!

On the evening of 12 April, we learned that MacArthur had issued orders for us to go to Australia. At about 0400 hours on 14 April, I was called to the field and told that they had repaired the B-17, which had been struck by Japanese bombers. They asked me to please step lively and get aboard because they wanted to take off. Numerous delays postponed our takeoff until dawn was beginning to break. At the last moment, one of our boys came over and told me that they had a plaintext message from 'Foto Joe' [a Japanese reconnaissance plane] that he and six fighters were

patrolling south of Mindanao. I gave the pilot this information and we took off. We had no sooner cleared the field when two float planes came in. Although we were heavily loaded and slow, they did not attack because we had guns. We flew east from Del Monte and headed south, giving Mindanao a wide berth. All looked well until one engine started pumping oil and had to be shut down. We were about forty-five minutes out at the time, with nineteen people aboard, and two full bomb bay tanks. With the Japs at Del Monte, there was no question of going back. We pumped gas into the wing tanks as rapidly as possible, and soon had the plane fairly well trimmed. Then another motor started throwing oil. Power was reduced on this engine and the other two were stepped up, and we worked our way to Darwin, Australia, with all three engines working on feather edge. When we landed, more than one strong man kissed the ground.

When we arrived in Brisbane, Australia, the next evening, I experienced culture shock when I suddenly burst into a lighted street with streetcars, people in civilian clothes, and lighted shops with things to sell. The shock was so great that it actually made me dizzy. I checked into a hotel and took stock of my possessions – two cotton uniforms (both on, both dirty), a pistol in my belt, a briefcase full of secrets, and about an inch of beard. I treated myself to a meal of tropical fruit and had a slow, hot bath. Flying south to Melbourne the next day, I reported to Joe Scherr, who let me cry in his beer, and he told me that things were bad, but that everyone was doing the best they could.

Colonel Brown served with distinction in the Central Bureau. He was part of the 126th Signal Radio Intelligence (SRI) company, the first U.S. intercept unit to be operational in Australia.

Traveling from Stateside

Charles E. Girhard obtained a B.A. in chemistry from the University of Illinois in June 1940. During his college studies, he also completed Reserve Officer Training Corps (ROTC) training and was introduced to cryptology. Upon graduation, he had two weeks of active duty at the munitions building in Washington, D.C., working under Dr. Sinkov in the Italian section. He obtained a teaching assistant job at Pennsylvania State University and planned to obtain a master's degree. These plans were interrupted in January 1941 when he was called up for active duty. Charles Girhard was part of the first group of officers to come to Central Bureau directly from the U.S. His experience sheds light on the logistics of transporting troops over great distances during the war.

Major Charles E. Girhard
(Source: S.I.S. Record)

I received orders dated 1 April 1942 that I was going to Australia. In those days, there was no such thing as volunteering. I was given about three or four days' notice of this move to Australia. I was part of the first contingent to go to Central Bureau, which consisted of three other officers: Larry Clark, Robert Holmes, and Hawkins, and eight enlisted men. When I left the munitions building, I just knew I was going to MacArthur's headquarters. There was no briefing about our assignment.

We flew to San Francisco on a commercial flight. That leg was the easy part of the trip. We checked into the Presidio base and ran into our first problem. We had secret orders, which you could not show to anyone. Secret orders gave you priority in transportation, but you couldn't tell anyone where you needed to go. Someone made an excerpt copy of the orders and we got that one straightened out. The next hurdle was for the Army to figure out how to get us to Australia.

I was surprised that I was the only one in our group who was told to report to Hamilton Field on the following day after we arrived in San Francisco. I found that I was one of two passengers boarding an LB30 cargo plane full of machine guns and aircraft parts. My companion, a tech representative who was going to help the Australians set up machine guns, and I had to sit in the bomb bay. There was no heat in the plane so we had several blankets. It was still very cold. Since the plane was about five tons overweight, it was a long, slow trip. It took us fifteen hours just to get to our first stop in Hawaii. We had the same Australian crew for the entire trip. While the crew was resting, I was lucky because I got to tour Hawaii for six hours.

For the next several days, we flew during the day and spent the night at various Pacific islands. Our next stop was Christmas Island. Christmas Island was about twenty miles wide and had nothing but coconut trees on it. I remember that stop because there was a small detachment of men who were thrilled to see us. They had not seen a newspaper in six weeks. No ship had called for about two months so they had no letters from home. Those poor fellows were just glad to see someone from civilization.

Next we stopped at Canton Island, which was nothing but an airstrip surrounded by a lagoon. We also stopped at Fiji. Finally, we reached Sydney.

My orders were so secret that they just said to report to MacArthur's headquarters. Where was MacArthur's headquarters? Eventually I found out and got myself on a train to Melbourne. When I got there, Colonel Joe Scherr introduced me to everything. At last, Colonel Scherr took me to the mansion on 225 Main Street, Central Bureau's head-quarters for the Melbourne period.

Girhard established the cryptographic section at Central Bureau and served there with distinction for the remainder of the war.

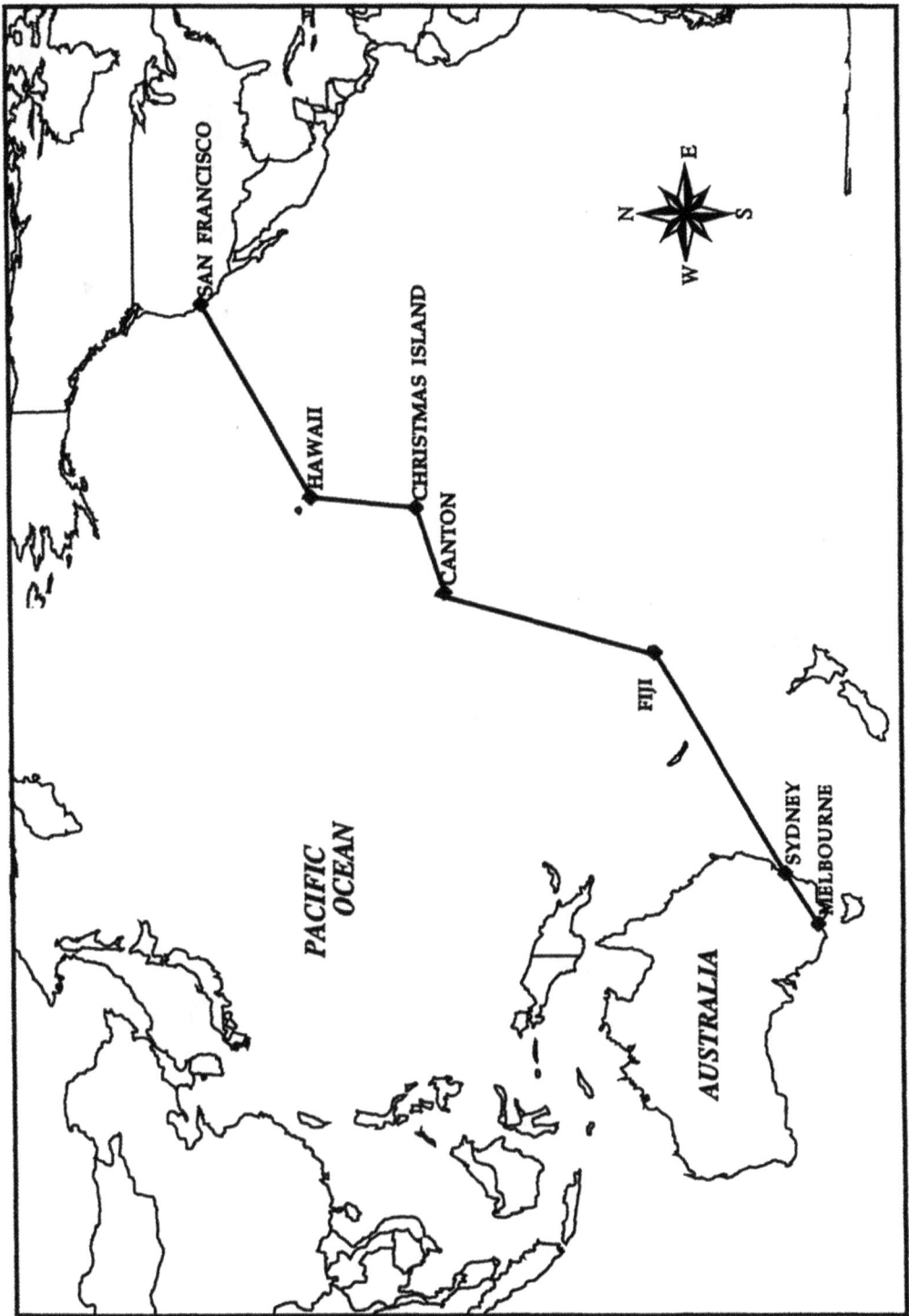

Charles Girhard's travel route

Chapter 2
Challenges at Central Bureau Field Section

The first link in gathering COMINT is the intercept unit. As Lieutenant Colonel A. W. Sandford, one of the assistant directors of Central Bureau and an AIF commander, said: "We are in the hands of the operators." The field sections under Central Bureau's operational control were vital to the success of providing intelligence to the Southwest Pacific theater. There were three types of field units under Central Bureau's operational control. They were Australian Army Wireless Sections (AAWS), RAAF wireless units, and American SRI companies. The AAWS began operations in 1942. The RAAF units were not ready for action until 1943. These units took over the Japanese air-ground problem, leaving the Japanese army problem to the AAWS. There were four American SRI companies in the theater, the 126th, the 112th, the 125th, and the 111th. The 126th SRI, which had come to Brisbane in 1943, had the longest period of service in the the-

Lieutenant Colonel Alastair W. Sandford
(Source: S.I.S. Record)

ater. The American platoon that came from Corregidor to Melbourne in April 1942 was incorporated into this company. The remaining three companies were not ready for action until 1944. The American SRI companies served primarily in Hollandia, New Guinea, Leyte, and San Miguel, Luzon, the Philippines.

Japanese air-ground communications were the most lucrative sources of information for field sections. One of the first systems that field units used to predict Japanese attacks were weather broadcasts. Analysts deduced that whenever a large Japanese station such as Tokyo, Truk, Dublon Island, or Rabaul, New Britain Island, broadcasted the weather for an Allied territory, that territory would be bombed. By calculating the difference between the time of origin of the broadcast and the time of' the previous air raid on that territory, analysts predicted numerous Japanese attacks in New Guinea and the Solomons with great reliability. It is interesting to note that Central Bureau and its field sections were responsible for intercepting and decrypting Japanese navy air-ground communications. The Navy handled all other Japanese naval communications itself.

Central Bureau read Japanese army air-ground communications almost continuously from 1942 until the end of the war because they were able to learn enough about the codes from code books captured in India. By reading air-ground communications, field units were able not only to provide air raid warnings, predict times of Japanese attacks, and identify concentrations of land forces but also to provide schedules of convoy movements because Japanese reconnaissance planes escorted their convoys.

Sometimes the field unit was the sole source of Allied intelligence. A notable example was the identification of the resupply convoy bringing enemy reinforcements to Ormoc on the west coast of Leyte in 1944. With this advanced notice, the U.S. sank five transports, damaged their escorts, and destroyed needed equipment and supplies. The Japanese Army's Twenty-sixth Division never had a chance to show its fighting ability on Leyte.

Most intercept units were always on the move. They had to keep up with the advance of the Allied troops to provide support. They had to keep looking for better spots to improve reception and set up direction finding apparatus. Intercept units were spread throughout the Southwest Pacific theater, from Perth, Australia, in the west to the Solomon Islands in the east, and from Mornington, Victoria, in southern Australia to the Philippines in the north. It is interesting to note that while the majority of intercept units were staffed entirely by men, there were some exceptions. Two intercept units, located at Mornington and at Perth, were staffed by women in the Australian Women's Auxiliary Service (AWAS). Another unit at Townsville, Queensland (Australia), was staffed in part by operators from the Women's Australian Auxiliary Air Force (WAAAF).

The recollections that follow from Australian representatives of wireless units and wireless sections cover 1942 to 1943. The best description of the war in the Southwest Pacific theater in 1942 is that it was a learning experience for MacArthur and the Allies. Central Bureau laid a solid foundation of intercept units, but it took time to develop a base of information. At the start of 1943, the Japanese and the Allies were at a stalemate in New Guinea. Each side had established strongholds in the area, and neither could oust the other. By the end of 1943, the Allies had significant victories such as the Battle of the Bismarck Sea and the destruction of the

Japanese air force at Wewak, New Guniea. However, MacArthur's ground campaign had advanced only 300 miles, which is about one-third of the way along the northern New Guinea coast. Manila was definitely a long way off.

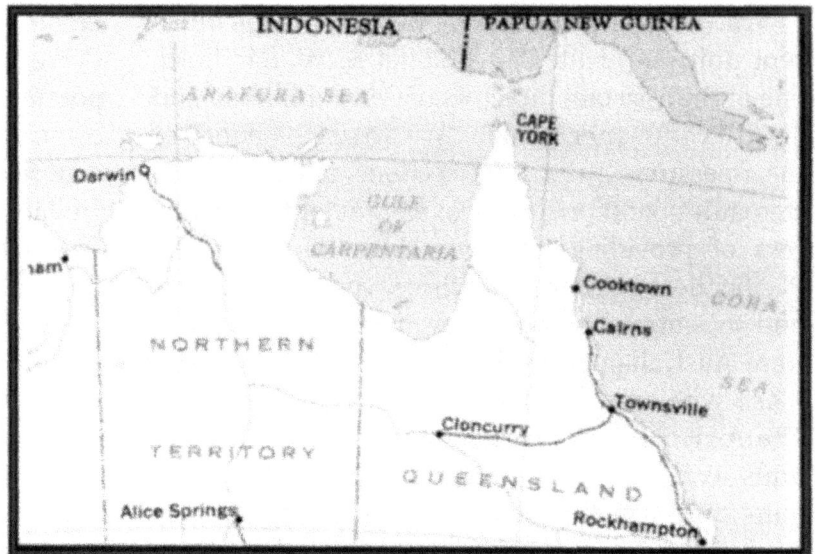

Australian intercept operators kept track of the Japanese activities in neighboring New Guinea.

Mastering Japanese Intercept

Prior to World War II , the Royal Australian Air Force (RAAF) had little experience in COMINT. The RAAF conducted its first class for Japanese intercept operators in July 1941. It established an administrative intelligence unit in the fall of 1941. Wing Commander H. Roy Booth, formerly a solicitor, was the commander of this new section of the RAAF. Booth was also one of Central Bureau's assistant directors. By July 1942, the number of RAAF intercept operators had grown from seven to twenty-nine. Several skills were needed to intercept Japanese traffic, and it took some time to recruit and train enough personnel to meet the demand for operators. In March 1942, the RAAF set up an intercept station at Townsville. The group at this station was renamed One Wireless Unit (1WU) on 25 April 1942. 1WU was the first intercept unit that came under Central Bureau operational control. Jack Bleakley, a member of 1WU, gives an excellent description of the complexities faced by intercept operators who had to copy Japanese traffic. Bleakley was born in Melbourne, Australia. He joined the RAAF in 1942 and served with 1WU in Townsville in 1942, in Port Moresby in 1943, and in Nadzab, New Guinea; Owi Island, and Biak, New Guinea, in 1944. In 1945, Bleakley served with 5WU in the Philippines. After leaving the RAAF in 1946, Bleakley resumed his banking career. The following recollections were taken from *The Eavesdroppers* by Jack Bleakley (Australia, 1992).

Wing Commander Henry Ray Booth
(Source: S.I.S. Record)

SIGINT personnel in the Southwest Pacific theater had unique problems that our counterparts in Europe did not face. We had to contend with the complexities of the Japanese language, and we had to learn Kana, a new Morse code system. Kana Morse signals were based on the forty-six phonetic sounds (plus twenty-five other sound changes) of the Japanese language, using their Katakana syllabary. The Japanese chose Katakana because it fulfilled their military requirements for expression of foreign words such as placenames, borrowed from the Western world, as well as the syllabary used to write

and phonetically pronounce traditional Japanese words. Allied intercept operators had a huge task. They had to learn the seventy-one Kana Morse symbols as opposed to the twenty-six-letter alphabet of the international code. They had to learn to completely ignore the international code. They also had to cope with the speed of Japanese operators. Speeds of forty to fifty words per minute were commonplace.

To cope with the speed problem, a shorthand system was devised to record Kana symbols onto the message pads. Therefore, operators had to learn both Kana and the shorthand system for recording it. The third step in the task was to write down the anglicized form of the Kana that was copied.

Of course, enemy signals and messages had to be copied accurately the first time. There was no way one could ask the Japanese for repeats. Inaccurate copy could foul up the cryptologists' work, rendering codebreaking difficult or even impossible. We were especially aware that missed signals or messages could lead to loss of lives. The skill level that the Kana operators achieved was truly remarkable. Later events in the war confirmed their talent.

The Paradox of Life at a Field Site

In contrast to the RAAF, Australian army units had considerable intercept experience in 1942. They acquired this knowledge from the British, whom they assisted in the Middle East and Africa. Australian army intercept units were called wireless sections. Wireless sections were self-contained units because each one had an intelligence section

The Katakana Chart: M. - KANA   C. PHONETIC   B. MORSE   D SHORTHAND

COLUMN / LINE	A	I	U	E	O
SINGLE VOWEL	ア A(Ñ)	イ I(A)	ウ U	エ E(N)	オ O(S̄)
K	カ KA(L)	キ KI(T)	ク KU(V)	ケ KE(Y)	コ KO(—)
S	サ SA(Z)	シ SHI(V)	ス SU(O)	セ SE(>)	ソ SO(ā)
T	タ TA(N)	チ CHI(F)	ツ TSU(P)	テ TE(ʌ)	ト TO(Ē)
N	ナ NA(R)	ニ NI(C)	ヌ NU(H)	ネ NE(Q)	ノ NO(J̄)
H	ハ HA(B)	ヒ HI(Ξ)	フ HU(Z)	ヘ HE(E)	ホ HO(D)
M	マ MA(X)	ミ MI(ʌ)	ム MU(T)	メ ME(=)	モ MO(√)
Y	ヤ YA(W)		ユ YU(X)		ヨ YO(M)
R	ラ RA(S)	リ RI(G)	ル RU(J)	レ RE(O)	ロ RO(Ā)
W	ワ WA(K)		ン N (+)		ヲ WO(J)

Part of the Katakana Morse code used by the Japanese military

made up of traffic analysts, cryptanalysts, and linguists. These Australian wireless sections handled the bulk of the intercept work during the early years of Central Bureau.

Major Geoffrey Ballard, a member of the AIF, was part of Central Bureau at its inception. In January 1942, he was called home from the Middle East to defend the homeland, along with all Australians who were serving overseas. Ballard held numerous posts at Central Bureau. The following recollections cover his experience with Fifty-one Wireless Section, the first Australian army intercept unit deployed to the field by Central

Bureau. Ballard underscores the importance of the work performed in the field and gives the reader a taste of some of the challenges they faced. These recollections were taken from Ballard's book, *On Ultra Active Service* (Australia, 1991).

After my promotion to captain, I was assigned to Darwin, Australia, in January 1943. I relieved Lieutenant Knoby Clark as head of the intelligence component of the Fifty-one Wireless Section. Life at Darwin was a paradox, for it was both very exciting and very boring.

Our work was certainly both challenging and exciting. The role of a field unit was to give local commanders operational intelligence of immediate value, give warning of impending air raids, advise on concentrations of enemy aircraft, ships, and land forces, and intercept certain high-grade traffic for research and decoding by Central Bureau. Initially our army wireless sections were responsible for covering both enemy air activities and ground operations. The RAAF wireless units eventually took over the Japanese air problem. We not only provided information to the forces at Darwin, but also alerted our sister intercept unit, Fifty-five Wireless Section, located at Port Moresby, New Guinea, of impending enemy movements toward New Guinea. We learned to read the signs of impending air attacks. For instance, when the Japanese moved aircraft from rear bases to forward bases, we knew they were getting ready for a bombing raid. Another indicator was the use of transport planes as escorts for the bombers as they moved to forward bases. When transports were abroad, we knew the

bombers were coming on an attack mission. Traffic analysts had to become good record keepers. Any increase in the volume of traffic was also a good indication of impending attack. During the first half of 1943, we were concerned about self-protection because Darwin was a frequent bombing target for the Japanese. In the latter half of the year, most of our air raid warnings were for New Guinea. The contributions of traffic analysts to the war effort were numerous. Inferences drawn from traffic analysis were used to accurately predict both impending attacks and information on order of battle and strategic intelligence. Traffic analysis often provided the first tip-off on Japanese plans for troop deployment. For instance, in August 1943, traffic analysts noted the increase in activity at Wewak [on the east coast of New Guinea]. Therefore, traffic analysts inferred that the Japanese were moving their headquarters from Rabaul in [Papua, New Guinea] to Wewak. This information enabled the U.S. Air Force to destroy 201 aircraft in two days.

Sometimes inferences from traffic analysis could predict information before message content was decoded and translated. Some outstanding examples of this type of prediction occurred in 1944. Three weeks before confirmation by ULTRA, traffic analysts predicted the Japanese intention to reinforce Morotai, [an island between New Guinea and the Philippines]. On 1 November 1944, traffic analysts predicted that the Japanese Southern Army planned to move its headquarters from Manila to Saigon. This prediction was first inferred because traffic analysts noted that the Burma Army was signalling through Saigon directly to Tokyo instead of signalling Tokyo through Manila. Our Allied liaison in India passed this information to Central Bureau. Subsequent evidence from a 15 November message confirmed this prediction. The message stated that Southern Army headquarters would begin to move to Saigon starting 17 November. All messages should be sent to both Manila and Saigon through 25 November.

One of the most exciting things that occurred during my stay in Darwin from January 1943 to January 1944 was the capture of a new code book from a Japanese bomber that crashed just west of our camp. Since we were instructed to send the book to Central Bureau by the next safe hand delivery [courier], which happened to be the next morning, we spent the night hand-copying as much of the book as we could. We were really encouraged by how much of the code we had recovered by ourselves.

While our work was exciting and challenging, there was little else in the way of diversion at Darwin. The Darwin post was at best flat and boring for our section. Marooned in the bush nearly 3,000 kilometers from the nearest city, we had to learn the lessons of survival and keep sane by our own wits. It was a stern, unnatural man's world with no local inhabitants to visit, no shops or towns to frequent, and no women to see. For a change of pace, the men made jewelry from plane wreckage, grew gardens (especially vegetables), and made pets of the kangaroos and parrots in the area.

Since I recognized that our major enemy was boredom, I looked for ways to motivate the men and keep them on their tasks. With permission from Central Bureau, at my discretion, I conducted a review of the week's work every Saturday morning. I told the men how many air raid warnings we had issued and how many Japanese planes were shot down because of our information. I felt that the 'need-to-know' principle of security did not apply to this situation. I wanted to show the men the importance of our work and how we fit into the big picture of the war effort. Attendance at these sessions was voluntary. They were very popular and helped us maintain team spirit, good morale, and productivity.

My year at Darwin was a sobering, maturing experience. Although the days were monotonous, I still remember the comradeship and storytelling. We shared a great deal of one another's thoughts and views and learned to appreciate and accept one another – warts and all.

On the Move in New Guinea

The following recollections by members of Fifty-five Wireless Section were collected by Geoffrey Ballard in his book *On Ultra Active Service*.

In September 1942, Fifty-five Wireless Section moved from Bonegilla, Victoria, Australia, to Port Moresby, New Guinea, the primary focus of Japanese activity. Today this area is known as Papua New Guinea. It lies

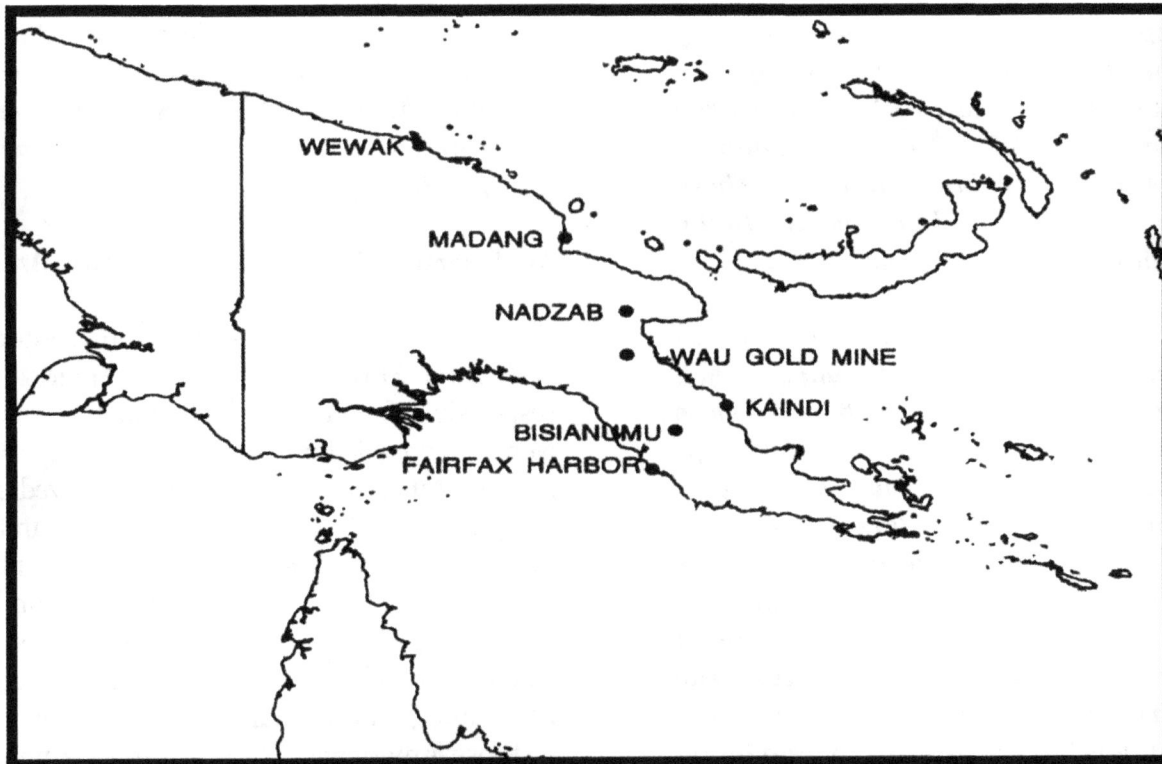

Detachments from the Fifty-five Wireless Section found themselves
in the rugged terrain of eastern New Guinea in 1943.

just south of the equator and is a mountainous region of rain forests. Describing life in New Guinea as rugged is an understatement. Throughout 1943 and in most of 1944, MacArthur pushed the Japanese out of New Guinea and pressed on to the Philippines. Intercept units kept pace with the Allied troops to provide intelligence. Detachments found themselves living in a wide variety of situations.

Fairfax Harbor in Port Moresby was the first location for intercept by Fifty-five Wireless Section. We had quite a welcome to New Guinea. During our very first night as we camped out in the open by Murray Barracks, three Japanese bombers paid us a visit. Luckily, the bombs fell well wide of their mark. The calm of such old stagers as our commander,

Captain John Vasey, set a fine example for the troops. Our job in the coming months was to keep the sets on no matter what else was happening around us. We began work the very next day and for an entire year, day in and day out, never lost contact with the enemy. Fairfax Harbor was a good location. We lived in tents and were away from the main flow of road traffic. The set room even had louvered walls for ventilation. In January 1943, Fifty-five Wireless Section moved out from Fairfax Harbor to a specially prepared site known as Seven Miles. This site was on a hill between the Seven Miles strip and Wards Drome.

Detachments from Fifty-five Wireless Section found themselves working in interesting locations. A few days after our arrival at Fairfax Harbor in

September 1942, a detachment of about fifteen men moved up the mountain range to Bisianumu near the Rouna Falls. They set up shop on the edge of a rubber plantation. These 'mountain boys' did not return to the unit until December 1942.

When Wau gold mine was recaptured from the Japanese in January 1943, a detachment from Fifty-five Wireless Section set up an advanced intercept point in the area. Two contingents spent six-month intervals at Wau. The only way into Wau, which is approximately 180 miles north of Port Moresby, was by air. Landing at Wau was memorable because the airstrip was hewn out of the rain forest, forcing the aircraft to land on an upward sloping hill. The site was 600 meters up from the Wau airstrip at Kaindi on the Edie Creek. Since the Japanese were still active in nearby Salamaua and conducted air raids over Wau, we put our set room underground to avoid a direct hit. We dug an enormous hole in an abandoned barn and constructed a set room that could accommodate four operators at a time. Rations for Kaindi were flown in once a week. If the weather was bad or there were frequent Japanese air raids, we just tightened our belts a few notches for a day or two.

The detachment was able to gather valuable intelligence. For instance, it was the only source of information that detected the movement of a regiment of the Japanese Forty-first Division from Wewak to Madang [100 miles southeast of Wewak]. By October 1943, it was time for the detachment to move on. The electrical storms of the rainy season made

reception difficult. The war front was now beyond the detachment's reach. We flew north to Nadzab, New Guinea, ready to take up our next position.

An American Perspective on Traffic Analysis

Although there was a general division of labor at Central Bureau whereby the Americans were responsible for cryptanalysis and the Australians were responsible for traffic analysis, as the war progressed, Americans became more involved in traffic analysis. The U.S. sent its own intercept units to the theater. American SRI companies served primarily in Hollandia, New Guinea, Leyte, and San Miguel, Luzon, the Philippines. Some Americans worked side by side with the Australians at intercept sites performing traffic analysis. Cecil Corey was one of those Americans. He has a unique perspective on the relationship between Americans and Australians.

After graduating from the University of Georgia with a bachelor's degree in agriculture, Cecil Corey was drafted by the Army in the fall of 1941. After studying at the cryptologic school in Vint Hill Farms, Virginia, Corey became a military trainer for the school. In January 1944, Corey attended officer candidate school (OCS) and joined Central Bureau in October 1944. Upon leaving the Army in December 1946, Corey worked for the National Security Agency's (NSA) predecessor agencies, the Army Security Agency (ASA) and the Armed Forces Security Agency (AFSA), and then for NSA. Corey's Central Bureau experiences were a good preparation for his NSA career. He made invaluable contributions in communications security (COMSEC). Corey retired in 1982.

By the time Corey arrived in Australia in October 1944, the Allies had pushed their way through New Guinea, forcing the Japanese to either vacate the area or abandon their garrisons. MacArthur then began his conquest of the Philippines. Since MacArthur believed that a general headquarters should be close to the war front, he moved from Brisbane, Australia, to Hollandia, New Guinea, in August 1944. In November 1944, Central Bureau established a forward echelon at Hollandia to provide proper support to MacArthur. The pace of the war kept increasing. The Japanese were still formidable opponents, and they were determined to fight to either victory or death.

Some people have definite career goals and meticulously plan to reach each goal. Not me! My career developed partly by acquiring unique experience and partly by being at the right place at the right time. For example, my selection for cryptologic training at Vint Hill was pure luck. Although I had ROTC training in college, I was not commissioned as an officer because I failed the physical for being underweight. However, my ROTC experience made it possible for me to become a military skills instructor at Vint Hill.

When I first arrived at Vint Hill, it was still a farm. All of the important activities took place in the barn, even though it still had cow manure in it. I still remember my first interview with Sergeant Mason, who was trying to determine how much French I knew. It took place in a hay loft still loaded with hay. I made wonderful friends at Vint Hill who would influence my whole life.

When I arrived at Central Bureau Brisbane in 1944, my military occupational specialty was code compiler. [Harry] Larry Clark, who was second in command to Sinkov, decided that I should become a traffic analyst because Central Bureau did not do code compilation. I was sent up to Hollandia, New Guinea, as part of the Central Bureau forward echelon. The Australians were in charge of this unit.

When I arrived at Hollandia, Major Stan (Pappy) Clark was in charge and Captain Don Englis had operational responsibilities, such as issuing reports. Pappy Clark trained us by pairing us up with an experienced Australian corporal or sergeant. My training partner was Sergeant Mos Williams. After the war, Mos Williams eventually became [an assistant director] of the Australian SIGINT organization, Defence Signals Directorate [DSD]. Some of the American second lieutenants resented being trained by nonofficers. Some of them also felt that U.S. resources were winning the war and we did not need the Australians. Therefore many of the Americans goofed off in Hollandia.

I learned a great deal from Mos Williams and the other Australians.

Lieutenant Colonel [Harry] Larry Clark
(Source: S.I.S. Record)

They were very experienced, and I had a lot to learn. I admired their enthusiasm for their work and enjoyed their war stories about their Middle East experiences. In Hollandia, we intercepted Japanese army mainline communications. I learned to recover callsigns, reconstruct nets, and look for new sources of traffic.

At Hollandia, I was the only American that the Australians trusted to be in charge of a net because they recognized me as a professional. All of our nets were named after animals. My net was called 'yak'. I worked on Chinese traffic, which proved to be insignificant to the war effort. As I gained the trust and respect of the Australians, I became a liaison between the Australians and Americans.

When we moved to San Miguel in 1945, we were located on a sugar plantation. The intercept site at San Miguel never became fully operational because the war ended. I had some involvement in Olympic and Coronet, the plans for invading Japan. The duty of front-line support for the invasion was to be handled by the 126th SRI company. I was to be one of its officers. With the dropping of the atomic bomb in August 1945, the war ended, making the invasion plans unnecessary.

I did not have enough points to go home because of my late arrival to Australia. Colonel Sinkov appointed me the coordinator for radio intelligence for the Pacific. I was finally able to go home late in the summer of 1946. I was able to get on a ship by volunteering to take some SIGABAs home. [A SIGABA was a machine used to send encrypted communications.] The ship was bound for San Francisco. Unfortunately, the ship was rerouted through the Panama Canal eventually ending up at Bayonne, New Jersey, on the east coast. Then I had to take care of the SIGABAs until I could work out a way to get them back to Arlington Hall. The traffic analysis knowledge that I acquired through my Central Bureau experience opened the door to an exciting, challenging career.

TRAFFIC CONTRIBUTION OF INDIVIDUAL FIELD SECTIONS

FOR JUNE 45.

SECTIONS.	MESSAGES.
U.S.Army Sections.	
111 SRI Company	11197
112 " "	4922
125 " "	12127
126 " "	37156
	65402
Aust.Army and Canadian Army Wireless Sections.	
Aust.Special Wireless Group	13544
" " " " Det.A	7195
Canadian Special Wireless Group	27949
	48688
RAAF Wireless Units.	
3 Wireless Unit	3466
4 " "	2212
5 " "	2210
6 " "	4317
Central Bureau Training Group (RAAF)	634
	12839
GRAND TOTAL	126929

Central Bureau collected an astonishing amount of intelligence from the Japanese.
(Appendix C, Central Bureau World War II Technical Reports)

Chapter 3
Cryptanalysts at Work in Central Bureau

Breaking into Japanese army codes was an arduous task. Prior to Pearl Harbor, the U.S. did not study Japanese army codes because the emphasis was on Japanese diplomatic codes. Therefore, during the war there was no continuity of background knowledge to assist the cryptanalysts in their study of Japanese army codes. Japanese low-echelon army codes were especially difficult because army communications were vertical not lateral. Regiments had no direct communication with each other; they had to communicate through their division. Since each regiment had its own code and there was no lateral communication, Central Bureau could not get enough material to conduct in-depth studies to determine the pattern of construction of these codes. Low-echelon Japanese army communications were also difficult to intercept because these units transmitted on low power. A third difficulty with lower-echelon Japanese army communications was that they were enciphered with one-time pads so obtaining the enciphering key did not help the cryptanalyst. The Allies were stymied by these low-echelon codes throughout the war.

Beginning in March 1944, Central Bureau had considerable success in reading Japanese mainline army codes. The watershed in CBB history came with the capture of the entire cryptologic library of the Japanese army Twentieth Division in January 1944 at Sio, New Guinea. The Ninth Infantry Division of the Australian army found this material in a steel trunk that was buried near a stream bed. The Japanese, who were retreating westward to Madang, did not want the burden of carrying this trunk over the mountains. They could not burn the code books because conditions were too wet and Allied aircraft might detect the columns of smoke. An Australian engineer who was sweeping the area for mines located the steel trunk on 19 January

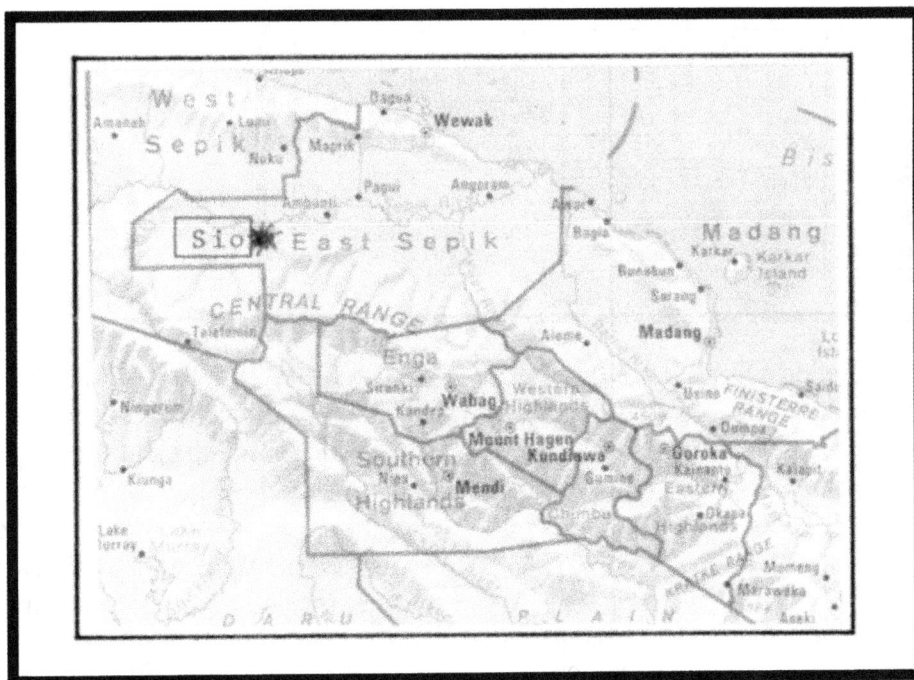

Sio, New Guinea, the site where the Australians captured the cryptologic library of the Twentieth Division of the Japanese army

人　名　（支　那）		（歐　米）
8368 工衛立煌	0768 ソ宋子文	
6797 閻錫山	3819 宋美齡	1691 「ウイルキー」
0601 才翁文瀬	5440 孫科	7341 「ウエーベル」
3325 王寵惠		3976 「オスメニア」
	1703 チ陳誠	9052 「カーチン」
8571 力何應欽	8492 陳立夫	0207 「ガンジー」
1264 郭泰祺	9186 陳果夫	8166 「キング」
3583 關麟徵	2058 陳濟棠	
6304 韓德勤	4200 陳銘樞	4648 「ゲーリング」
	7565 陳紹寬	6562 「スターク」
4558 キ居正	5293 沈鴻烈	0184 「スターリン」
2463 許崇智		9423 「スチムソン」
	2687 テ張發奎	1310 「スミス」
0487 コ孔祥熙	0005 張羣	3246 「セーヤー」
1073 顧維鈞	9670 趙承綬	2575 「ダフ・クーパー」
9546 顧祝同		6461 「チャーチル」
4491 胡適	5642 ト湯恩伯	8009 「トーマス」
2654 胡宗南	3921 唐生智	4378 「ドクー」
6180 吳鐵城	6685 杜律明	9647 「ニミツト」
		3752 「ノックス」
7598 シ周恩來	3673 ハ白崇禧	2980 「ハル」
1860 周鐘嶽	2126 ヘ馮玉祥	5458 「バーモ」
0982 朱德	3303 モ毛澤東	6236 「ヒツトラー」（ヒ総統）
9759 朱紹良	7442 ユ愈飛鵬	0588 「ビブン」
3145 朱家驊	8795 ヨ余漢謀	1769 「ボバム」
7071 徐永昌	3189 ラ羅卓英	7284 「マーシアル」
		2395 「マック・アーサー」
7116 セ蔣介石	0892 リ李宗仁	6663 「ムツソリーニ」
4233 商震	4143 李濟琛	4592 「モロトフ」
7925 盛世才	5709 龍雲	3460 「ルーズベルト」
9849 邵力子	7688 劉峙	
8885 薛岳	8650 林森	
1972 錢大均		

A page from an original Japanese code book captured in 1944 or 1945. The Sanbo Hanbo Rikugun Angosho Yon Go (General Staff Army Code Book, fourth edition) is a high-level code book with an encoding and decoding section that was used to both send and receive messages. Page 33, Chines Europene Surnames, is taken from Section 1, Organizational Listings, of the code book. In this system, 6236 stands for MacArthur, and 3460 stands for President Roosevelt. (Explanation and translation provided by Dr. Ed Drea, Dept. of the Army.)

1944. The capture included the additive book, the substitution square, and the code book itself. One of the first messages that Central Bureau read from this code was from a Japanese lieutenant stating that all of the Twentieth Division's code books had been destroyed.

The following recollections by Charles E. Girhard, Joseph E. Richard, Abraham Sinkov, and John J. Larkin represent the views of both officers and enlisted personnel, as well as those who worked at Central Bureau throughout the war and those who joined the war effort later on. They paint a picture of the enormity of the tasks that these cryptanalysts faced. Breaking the Japanese army codes, while slow and arduous, had its exciting moments. The cryptanalysts functioned as a team and stuck to the tasks at hand, day after day and year after year, and achieved remarkable success.

The Key to Success Was Teamwork

Charles E. Girhard went to Central Bureau in April 1942 to establish its cryptologic section. Not only was Mr. Girhard one of the first Americans to arrive at Central Bureau, but he also served with this organization throughout its existence. His perspective on our cryptologic effort during the war is an important one.

During Central Bureau's Melbourne period from April to September 1942, we made little progress on the Japanese army codes because we did not have enough traffic to study. It took some time for intercept units to become operational. We primarily worked on the Japanese naval air problem. Major Norman Webb, a British officer who escaped from Singapore, brought naval air messages with him. This was the main source of our study. All of our work was done by hand during this early period. We were fortunate because the IBM equipment arrived at Brisbane around the time when increased amounts of traffic were also available. Our first IBM room was the garage in the house on Henry Street. [When Central Bureau moved to Brisbane in September 1942, it was located in a two-story house on Henry Street. With the increase of personnel, these spaces were soon overcrowded. In late 1943 Central Bureau moved a few blocks down to Ascot Park, where huts were built to house its various sections.]

Cryptanalysis is a slow, gradual process of looking for patterns. Sometimes we would only be able to determine a placename because encoding of placenames was semisystematic. We were watchful for messages where the Japanese had to clarify a point. Such messages were written in the Chinese telegraph codes, which were already available to us. The first major progress that we made was the solution of the Japanese Army Water Transport Code in April 1943. Our big break

The first American SISers in Brisbane. Photo was taken at the Henry Street Headquarters.
(Source: S.I.S Record)

This was the SIS beachhead in Melbourne, first home of the original group. Why couldn't all Army camps look like this? (Source: S.I.S. Records)

came with the capture of the entire cryptographic library of the Japanese army's Twentieth Division in January 1944 at Sio, New Guinea. From my vantage point, the key to our success was teamwork.

There was excellent teamwork both within Central Bureau itself as well as between Central Bureau and other organizations. In Central Bureau, people shared information with each other. We were a small enough organization that people in different sections could talk to each other to solve problems. Two examples of this team approach were the coordination between the cryptanalysis section and the machine section, and coordination between the cryptanalysis section and the intercept section. As the supervisor of the cryptologic section, I spent much time showing the IBM people what our problems were and what we wanted to do to solve them. Major Zach Halpin, the head of the

IBM section, was able to rearrange punch cards so that we could sort traffic by time interval. Sorting traffic by time interval was important in finding the solution to the Japanese Army Water Transport Code. After the Sio capture, operators programmed IBM machines to strip off cipher and print both the code number and its accompanying meaning in Romaji. [Romaji is the Japanese system of writing foreign words in the Roman alphabet.] After the traffic analyst put the address on the message and the cryptanalyst checked the message to determine its indicator or its starting point in the additive book, the messages went to the IBM room where the operators punched up the additive. Arlington Hall turned to us for instructions in some of these uses of IBM equipment. Communication between the various branches within Arlington Hall was not as good as Central Bureau's internal communication.

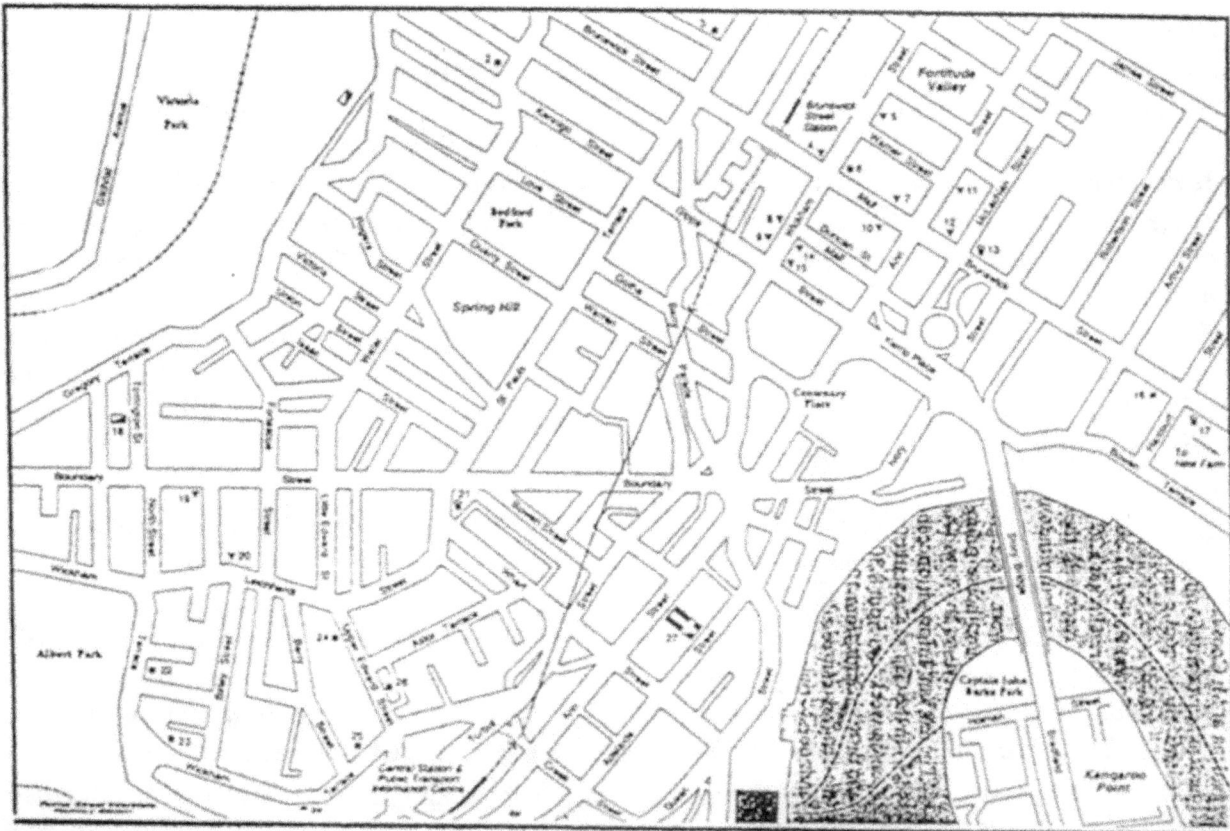

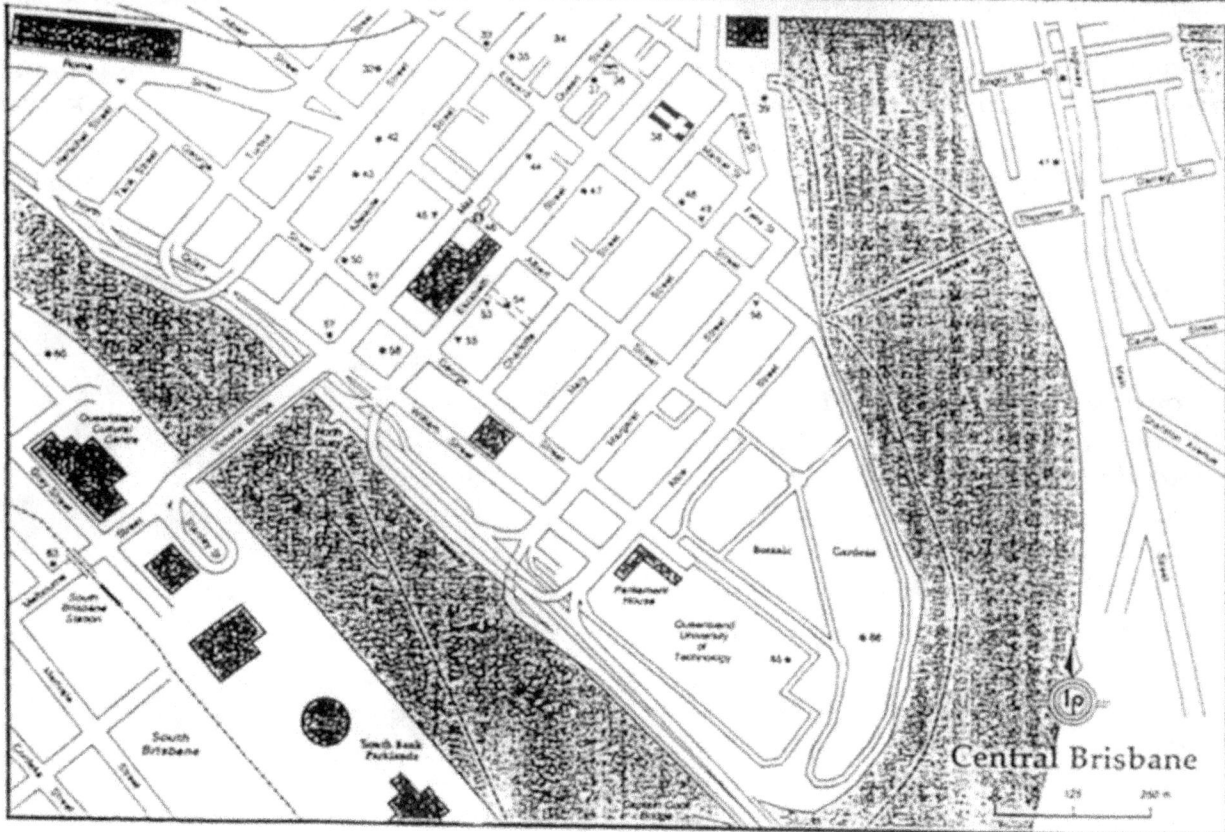

In Brisbane, Central Bureau was originally located in a house on Henry Street. It later moved to a new, larger facility at Ascot Park.

Because of good communication, traffic analysts knew how important it was for cryptanalysts to gain access to code instructions that the Japanese sent to their field units. Traffic analysts placed double coverage on Japanese circuits known to be used to transmit code instructions. Getting the key to a substitution square from the Japanese was an important time-saver for the cryptanalysts, which warranted double coverage of a circuit.

Central Bureau's good relationship with the Allied Translators Interpreters Service (ATIS) was not only rewarding to me personally but also was invaluable to the organization. [ATIS supported MacArthur's general headquarters by translating captured documents and interrogating Japanese prisoners.] Since members of ATIS accompanied the troops on their mission, I talked to them about the type of material we needed on a monthly basis. I learned of the Sio capture when an ATIS representative called me and asked me to come over and look at their find. ATIS was also located in Brisbane.

Captain [later Colonel] Hugh Erskine, head of Central Bureau's translation section, and I were so excited when we saw the Sio material that we took it to Central Bureau immediately. [Hugh Erskine later became an NSA senior and was the first National Cryptologic Representative to Europe.] What a mess! The books had been buried near a stream bed in a steel trunk that looked like a footlocker. There was so much mildew on the material that each page had to be dried in the large commercial cooking ovens in our kitchen. Our cleaning efforts were definitely worthwhile. The Sio material was a mainline Japanese army code used to communicate with many divisions. This material included the additive tables, the substitution squares, and the code book itself. From the time of the capture of the Sio material until the end of the war, we read approximately 2,000 messages a day.

Obtaining the actual Japanese codes gave us an opportunity to evaluate our own accuracy in recovering codes. It was rewarding to see how accurate we were. It was also instructive to see what kind of mistakes we made. There were numerous opportunities for error. The radio operator may not have heard the Morse correctly. It is interesting to note that the Australian radio operators copied code by hand and used the British shorthand style of writing numbers, which sometimes caused confusion. American operators used typewriters

**Lieutenant Colonel Hugh S. Erskine
(Source: S.I.S. Record)**

to copy code. Punch card operators sometimes made errors when transferring numbers. In additive cryptosystems, it is easy to get out of phase with the group count. If this happened, cryptanalysts would have to go back and look at the messages again after they had been punched up in the IBM room. Although these tasks were tedious, the men and women at Central Bureau recognized the importance of the job and put forth great effort to accomplish the mission.

I also went to Finschhafen with Hugh Erskine and Sergeant Schokal to review the material that was taken from the Yoshino Maru after the U.S. sank it off Aitape, on the northern coast of New Guinea, in May 1944. This barge was on fire for twelve hours before it went down. Once again, this too was a worthwhile trip because we obtained a new additive book. I am sure that Sergeant Schokal will remember this trip since he had to postpone his wedding to take it. The reconstruction of this registry occurred because of the hard work of both the cryptanalysis and photography sections of Central Bureau. We recovered 97 percent of the tables.

The best description of Central Bureau's relationship with Arlington Hall is friendly competition. There was competition in the sense that each wanted to recover a certain code first. We sent as much technical information and recoveries to Arlington Hall as we could. For instance, we sent all of the Sio material electrically to Arlington Hall. We also sent messages for them to work on because they had more personnel than we did.

Central Bureau did not have its own communications circuitry. We used the communications circuitry of the Australians to communicate with the intercept units and used the circuitry through MacArthur's headquarters for other needs. Approximately 80 percent of all the communications from MacArthur's headquarters to Washington was Central Bureau material for Arlington Hall. Dr. Solomon Kullback was the chief of operations at Arlington Hall. He and Dr. Sinkov had an excellent relationship. If there were any problems, Dr. Sinkov would send a message to Kullback, and Kullback would work on the problem right away. There was excellent teamwork between Central Bureau and Arlington Hall.

One exception to this teamwork approach was our relationship with the Navy. We did not work with our navy counterparts at FRUMEL. When Central Bureau was still located in Melbourne, Erskine and I went over to FRUMEL to talk to the Navy. When General Akin found out about our expedition, he ordered us to stay away from them. However, the Navy did send two translators to work with us to process the deluge of messages that resulted from the Sio capture. I don't know what General Akin's reasons were for this order. General Akin wanted to be in control. He kept many people away from us, including General Willoughby, MacArthur's G-2 section chief. Perhaps General Akin had security concerns.

With regard to security, I remember that we had a badge system at Ascot Park in Brisbane. You needed a badge for entrance, but it was not a picture

badge. Clearances were not empha-
sized because of the pressing need for
personnel. Late in the war, we got a
message from Washington stating
that Dr. Sinkov, Erskine, and I did not
have any clearances. They just
grandfathered us into the clearance
system. As MacArthur's chief signal
officer, General Akin was responsible
for providing any support that
Central Bureau needed. He did an
excellent job especially with logistics.
General Akin got the diver to go to the
Yoshino Maru to recover the code
book. He arranged for the planes so
that we could go to Finschhafen on
the northern coast of New Guinea to
look at this material. He also
arranged for all of Central Bureau's
moves. Moving from Brisbane,
Australia, to San Miguel, Luzon, in
the Philippines was quite an under-
taking. We had to copy all of our technical information so that one set
could be left at Brisbane and one set
could be taken to San Miguel. We
were afraid that material would be
lost, so copying, although time con-
suming, was essential. Moving the
various sections of Central Bureau
had to be carefully coordinated
because the war did not stop during
this relocation. Intercept units had to
move in stages so that coverage of
targets could be maintained. I kept
things going in Brisbane and did not
move to San Miguel until July 1945.

Although the war ended in August
1945, I did not leave for home until
Christmas Day 1945 because of transportation shortages. I remained on
active duty until 1948. I then worked
at NSA as a civilian and joined the
military reserves. My experiences at

Central Bureau were a very memorable part of my career.

The Joy of Discovery

Sergeant (later Warrant Officer) Joseph E.
Richard was drafted into the Army in April 1941. He
applied for cryptologic school while he was stationed at Fort Monmouth, New Jersey, attending
radio repair school. He attended the Army's cryptologic school, which was also located at Fort
Monmouth but did not finish the course because
people were needed for the war effort. After working in the munitions building in Washington, D.C.,
for several months, Richard left for Australia in
June 1942. He served at Central Bureau for the
remainder of the war. Mr. Richard played a leading
role in the discovery of the cryptanalytic solution to
the Japanese Army Water Transport Code. His
insight on that process and the day-to-day operations of Central Bureau is an important part of the
Central Bureau story.

I wanted an overseas assignment
because the Army was moving its
cryptologic operations from the
munitions building to Arlington Hall.
If I went to Arlington Hall, I would
have to go back to living in the barracks so I asked to go to England. The
Army sent me to Australia. The
Australians were glad to have us, and
I enjoyed my experience there very
much.

In 1942, we knew very little about the
Japanese army codes. While I was
still at the munitions building in
Washington, D.C., we didn't even
know which discriminants went with
which activity. For instance, we did
not know that 7890 was an army system or that 3366 was army/air. We
didn't find out the routing system
until September 1942. Arlington Hall
told Central Bureau how to identify

the 'from' and 'to' lines on messages and gave us a solution for place-names. I believe that Arlington Hall got this information from the Navy. There was an agreement between the services that if an army message came on navy circuits the Navy would turn it over to the Army. In the process of turning over army messages, the Navy gave Arlington Hall this information. For many months, we struggled to discover additional information.

Cryptanalysis was especially tedious in the early days of Central Bureau because we had to do everything by hand. At first, I worked on low-echelon army traffic. The study of these three-digit codes proceeded as follows: We did subtraction all day long and tried to match positions and messages with code groups. We worked in three-person teams. First we attempted to re-create the Japanese code book by making up composition books in which we wrote numbers consecutively from 1 to 999. Next, each team matched messages with groups of numbers in the composition book. By subtraction, we determined hits and wrote these hits in the composition book. For example, message five hit with message three at a slide of eight. After all the groups from a number of messages were entered in the composition books, other teams compared the entries looking for two or more hits between the same two messages at the same interval or slide (e.g., group 103 at position eleven in message five and position thirteen in message seven). The assumption was that the messages with the hits or the same groups occurring at the same interval might have used the same

additive. When the additive was removed and a difference between code groups resulted, you could establish a pattern difference. Such a comparison can be done quickly and accurately by IBM machinery once the message texts have been punched onto cards. We were very happy when the IBM equipment was finally operational. We finished this book of possibilities in the spring of 1943. We had worked on it by hand since my arrival in June 1942. Although we got some random hits, we made very little progress in breaking these codes.

I think that the IBM equipment became operational in March 1943. This equipment arrived at Sydney, Australia, but Central Bureau was never notified of its arrival. Sinkov sent Major Larry Clark to investigate what happened to our equipment. Fortunately, Clark found the equipment sitting on the dock. When the equipment finally reached Central Bureau, each machine had to be dismantled. We had to sand and tighten the relays so that the machine would be reliable. This extra work was necessary because of damage to the machinery caused by standing in the sea air for such a long time.

Breaking the Japanese Army Water Transport Code 2468 is an interesting story. In December 1942, I was very bored, frustrated, and depressed over a colleague's death. One day at the end of pistol instruction, which had been foolishly conducted right inside the building where we worked, a gun accidentally went off. John Bartlet, who happened to be sitting in the next room, was wounded and later died because the ambulance took such a long time to come. I wished I had just taken him to the hospital instead of waiting for the ambulance. I needed a change so I asked Sinkov if I could work on new traffic.

We sorted traffic by repeater groups. I noticed that the number five was never used. Sinkov showed me how to equate groups by subtraction to get down to the basic code. Sinkov also alerted Arlington Hall to this particular system of traffic.

I was fascinated by my discovery and began to come in on my own time at night to sort traffic by system. There were three systems: 2468, 7890, and 6666. After some time of sorting 2468, I noticed that the first number of the repeated group was random. I also noticed that in this system the repeated group was the second group of the text, but in other systems the repeated group was the third group in the text. (The repeated group indicates which system is in use.) Next I discovered that the system changed every few weeks. Major Zach Halpin set the IBM machines to sort by both group and time period. This was a difficult feat because key punch equipment had to be reconfigured to fit more information onto the cards. I started logging these messages to determine the exact time when the system changed so that I could sort them properly. Sinkov told Arlington Hall of the time period changes to 2468. Next I saw a correspondence between the first number of the group in front of the repeated group and the first digit of the repeated group. After writing out the tables of numbers, I found that all digits had just three digits after them.

I had three columns or tables because there were three different periods.

Clark made additional observations. He saw a correspondence between the first and second group after the repeated group. He also discovered several doublets. Clark made a list of all the possible doublets. I could not copy all of these doublets so I looked at single digits and saw that there was a ten-by-ten square. Clark deduced that the columns of numbers that I had should fit into this square. We spent the rest of the night trying to get the columns to fit into the square. We finished the task begun in December 1942 on 6 April 1943. What a great feeling to have finally found the solution.

Once again, Sinkov sent our discovery to Arlington Hall. They got back to us on 7 April 1943, stating that they had already made the same discovery.

Historians say that Central Bureau and Arlington Hall broke the 2468 code in parallel. I think that more of the credit belongs to Central Bureau because we alerted Arlington Hall that 2468 was a unique, separate system and that it should be sorted by time period.

We shared all kinds of information with Arlington Hall. Early in 1943, we began sending monthly progress reports to Arlington Hall and other cryptologic centers. I enjoyed working on these progress reports. We did a better job of including reference material than the other signals intelligence organizations did. For instance, whenever we published a

COMINT message about a new code system or changes to an old code system, we took the time to research all of the previous messages on that subject so that we could publish all of these messages. We also published working aids that we had developed in these progress reports. For instance, I made a map associating codes with the areas where they were used. I also devised a neat mathematical solution for recovering additive. I figured out that if we used the limitations of the square and went backward, we could get down to a single set of digits. This was faster and easier than matching each page of the additive book with the square. We made every effort to tell the complete story to all the cryptologic organizations.

After the 2468 solution, our work became more satisfying. Now that we understood that the Japanese used a square to encipher the starting point of 2468, we figured that other systems were developed in a similar manner. The solution of 2468 led to the solutions of 7890, its successor 5678, and to the solution of 6666. The 7890 and 5678 systems were mainline systems of communication between Japanese headquarters and army divisions. The 6666 system was a Japanese army air system. The work was still very difficult. The 2468 system remained difficult because we had to go through so much additive before we could read the indicator. By sorting and comparing resend messages and with the assistance of traffic analysis, we eventually determined that the Japanese chose the key for enciphering the indicator from a thousand group list, not from

the whole additive code book. This made our job more manageable.

We still had challenges. Since the Japanese radio operator sent messages only in sections of fifty code groups, all of the additive book had to be available. If we had a ten-part message, we needed ten pages of additive, not just two or three pages. Japanese radio operators also scrambled message parts and sent them randomly. Finding all of the parts to a message and getting them into the proper sequence was a chore. The operator further scrambled each individual message part so that the beginning of the section was never sent at the beginning of the transmission. Therefore, we had to determine where the section really began. When systems changed, we had to recover them again.

We were really busy after the capture of the Japanese code books at Sio, New Guinea, in January 1944. To accommodate additional personnel, Central Bureau had moved into expanded quarters at Ascot Park in Brisbane in late 1943.

We were organized into huts to facilitate the flow of work more efficiently. We read more and more messages all the time. When MacArthur was preparing to invade the Admiralties in the winter of 1944, I was on the team that decoded every message to or from the Admiralties. This task was not as exciting as I thought it would be. The Japanese did not reveal that much about their plans; most of the messages were about the importance of dying for the fatherland. However, we did warn the Allies that *the Japanese were sending many reinforcements to the Admiralties from Rabaul.*

Working as a cryptanalyst was boring and frustrating, but the joy of discovery made it an extremely worthwhile occupation. I left the Army in 1946. I continued my cryptologic career as a civilian and had several interesting overseas assignments with the Agency, including a return trip to Australia.

Putting Our Cryptanalytic Skills to the Test at Central Bureau – 1942-1945

Abraham Sinkov's lifelong dream was to become a mathematician. He obtained three mathematics degrees, his B.S. from City College of New York in 1927, his M.A. from Columbia University in 1929, and his Ph.D. from George Washington University in 1933.

One of the original disciples of William Friedman, Sinkov was a brilliant cryptanalyst. The breadth of Sinkov's experience included the establishment of the first intercept site outside the U.S., contributions in COMSEC, and, most importantly. contributions in cryptanalysis.

The Central Bureau period is the highlight of Abraham Sinkov's distinguished thirty-two-year cryptologic career. His managerial talents, interpersonal skills, and leadership qualities came to the forefront during this experience. Although General Akin was the director of Central Bureau, Sinkov managed the day-to-day responsibilities, which kept the organization functioning. Central Bureau participants credit Sinkov with maintaining a harmonious, cohesive atmosphere in the workplace. The Australian contingents were partners not rivals. Few Allied organizations from the World War II era ran as smoothly as Central Bureau did.

Abraham Sinkov

In 1946 Dr. Sinkov became the director of the communications security division of ASA. When the AFSA was established in 1949, Dr. Sinkov became the chairman of the communications security monitoring group. During the last ten years of Sinkov's career with the government, he made valuable contributions in both COMSEC and intelligence production at NSA. He retired in 1962.

I was selected commander of the 837th Detachment and arrived in Melbourne, Australia, in July 1942 to begin work at Central Bureau. MacArthur established Central Bureau on 15 April 1942. I can only speculate on why I was chosen for this position. Undoubtedly, one reason may be that work against the Japanese was considered a much more important subject than the work I did against Italian messages. One other possible reason might be that I was single at the time a decision was made to send me. [Solomon] Kullback and [Frank] Rowlett were married and had children. Marital status was a likely consideration if my superiors made the decision to send me before I married. As luck would have it, I happened to marry just a few weeks before I left for

Australia. The Australia assignment was my third tour of duty under General Akin. He was the head of Signals Intelligence Service [SIS] in Washington in the early 1930s and Mr. Friedman reported to him. I had two years in the Canal Zone with General Akin. He was a stern individual, but I found him quite easy to work with. I'm sure he had kindly feelings toward me. After all, what we produced was highly useful and desirable, and essentially reflected on him and his management. He was a hard worker, although somewhat taciturn. But I don't recall that there was any problem working under him.

General Akin rarely came to Central Bureau. We were located in a park about, oh, three or four miles from headquarters. I visited him regularly. I would come to his office in the headquarters building, also known as the AMP building. As MacArthur's chief signals officer, General Akin had additional responsibilities besides Central Bureau. All in all, I think that generally he was an easy person to work with.

During the first many months of our stay at Central Bureau, we received the intercepted material, organized it, studied it, and tried to seek cryptanalytic entries. It took quite a while before we made our first entry and began to get into any actual successful work. Central Bureau's mission was the whole range of Army communications including air traffic because apparently in the Japanese structure the Army was responsible for air traffic. In terms of cryptanalytic study, we had an air-ground section, a mainline army communica-tions section, and a water transport section because it too was a Japanese army responsibility. We studied both Japanese army and Japanese navy air-ground, but they were not two distinct sections. Because of his experience, the air-ground problem was under the control of Royal Naval Officer Captain Nave, who produced a good deal of useful intelligence. Central Bureau also tried to attack low-level traffic in the three-digit systems.

The problem with low-level traffic, tactical traffic actually, was availability. Tactical traffic was transmitted under low power. We had no intercept capability to obtain this traffic because we were not close enough. Just a handful of people worked with this traffic. They were headed by Professor Room, who was coopted from the University of Sydney, where he was head of the mathematics department. There wasn't a great deal of success accomplished against low-level traffic. The results obtained were essentially some traffic analytic results. There were not any cryptanalytic successes against low-level traffic, except in later years, when we had actual captured material. Then we could read some of the low-level traffic.

The Water Transport System deserves some special consideration because entry into this system was our first success. The Japanese designator for this system was 2468. We achieved this breakthrough solely by using cryptanalytic techniques. The cryptographic process was a process by which a message which had been encoded with a code book was then enciphered with an additive pad. Our initial break-in was to realize how the pad was being used. This discovery permitted us to start separating the material into portions that were related in that they used the same part of the book. We were gradually able to solve part of the book. Reconstruction of a code book is a lengthy complicated process. Our job was not over once we reconstructed the code book. The Japanese made regular changes to their additive book so we had to go through the whole process all over again.

Intelligence cannot be derived until the cryptanalyst makes a reasonable entry into the code book. Although the first entry into the Japanese Army Water Transport System was in April of 1943, Central Bureau started deriving intelligence from this system in the fall of 1943. When we finally got into the code book and produced decrypts, we found much useful information about transport activity, including the movement of troops and supplies to the various island installations. Many of the messages that we read in 2468 gave sailing schedules of their transports. These messages also usually gave expected noon positions of the transport for every day of an entire week until it reached its destination. This was most useful information. Submarine commanders were directed to a particular spot at a particular time, and, sure enough, they frequently found that there was a Japanese transport they could attack. Our successes were really quite significant since once we got to the point later on in the war when captured materials became available, our cryptanalytic problem was then

greatly simplified. One of our great delights was the Sio capture. The capture of the material at Sio, New Guinea, in January 1944, gave us access to the entire cryptographic library of the Japanese army's Twentieth Division. It certainly spared us a great deal of work. Central Bureau had an agreement with ATIS, the organization responsible for the handling of captured materials, that ATIS would turn over to Central Bureau any materials related to signals intelligence. Central Bureau had its own translators. After the Sio capture, one of our officers made a special trip to ATIS to obtain this material.

The question arises, could we [have broken] the four-digit mainline Japanese army codes if we [had] not captured the Sio material? I think if we had had enough material we would have broken these codes. There was a similarity to all of the Japanese army cryptanalytic systems. Once we developed the Japanese mind-set and knew how they worked, we could have been successful given a sufficient amount of intercepted material.

Obtaining the Japanese code book from the Yoshino Maru, a barge that the U.S. sank off Aitape [New Guinea], is an interesting story. One of our personnel read a message about the existence of this additive book and realized that even though the ship burned, the text might still be available if each page was not burned separately. General Akin arranged for a diver to retrieve the book. When Central Bureau received the book, it was a burned mass that was very difficult to deal with. We had a very competent officer named Holmes with a chemical background who was able to take this thing and reconstruct it page by page. After a certain amount of experimentation, Holmes directed us to coat each individual page with an alcohol solution. This process brought the writing into focus long enough to take a picture of it. Bit by bit we reconstructed the whole book.

To appreciate the enormity of our tasks, two points should be kept in mind. Even though we obtained captured material, we were never free from slow reconstruction and analysis work because we studied many systems. The captures did not cover all systems. A second point to consider is that readability varies. Solving a code message or a code system is different from solving a cipher. Normally when you solve a cipher, you can read the entire communication without any problem. In solving a code it's a process of little-by-little reconstruction of the book. It means that messages are readable only in part in the early stages and there will be gaps. The extent of the gaps will diminish as you get further and further into the code book.

The Japanese procedure, as I remember it, was simply this. First the message was encoded. The encoding produced a series of four-digit groups. Then, with a special signal that ended the message, [the encipherer] turned to a place in an additive book with page upon page of four-digit groups.

The encipherer was instructed by means of the special key group, which actually he selected in the process, to go to a particular part of the additive book and start copying from that particular part four-digit groups in order. [He wrote these numbers] under the four-digit groups of the code message. Next the process, which is sometimes called false addition, takes place.

False addition [today referred to as Modulus2] is a noncarrying addition. [This sum or result was what the operator finally transmitted as the message.] Remember, selecting which part of the additive book to go to was one which had a great deal of variation. It was a book of many pages. The keying procedure permitted starting anywhere on any one of these pages. From there on, we took the groups in order. It's basically a fairly secure method of communication.

But that was what started us. By knowing where in the additive book a particular message began its encipherment, we were able to put together messages which used the same portion of the additive book, and that depth of material then permitted us to make cryptanalytic progress. As time developed, our output increased tremendously because of both additional cryptanalytic successes and information from captured material.

Developing the Clues to Solve the Cryptanalytic Puzzle

One cryptanalyst, who chose not to be identified, described his experience at CBB this way:

I arrived in Brisbane, Australia, in the spring of 1944. I was assigned to Hut Fourteen. . . . Each hut had a work space for approximately thirty or forty people. Shortly after my arrival, Central Bureau went on round-the-clock shift work. I enjoyed my shift, which was 5:00 P.M. to 2:00 AM.

I was struck by the variety of people who worked at the Bureau. I think there was one New Zealander, ten Canadians, and about ten Britishers. I worked directly with two Australians [who] introduced me to the specifics of our daily tasks. Rank was not important. We knew we had a job to do and everyone just worked at it.

One of the Japanese army codes that I worked on was 6666. In this system, the first four code groups were of paramount importance. The first group gave the enciphering indicator for that particular message. The second group gave the page of the code book to use for the encipherment. The third group gave the column and row. Frequently, the last digit of the third group was the sum of the previous seven digits. The fourth group contained the group count for the message. Each message usually contained forty code groups. Since each digit in each group had been enciphered, we had to follow each digit through the square to find the correct composition of the group.

The Japanese provided us with helpful clues. Some clues were stylistic, while other clues came from the logistics of their distribution problems. Within the message itself, the Japanese used many stereotypic expressions or text repetitions. This repetition lessened our work. If the Japanese wanted to emphasize some-thing to make sure a word or number was understood, they used speller groups. These speller groups were always placed in parentheses. The text in parentheses often gave us the start we needed to break out the rest of the code.

Changing the codes presented a great problem for the Japanese as the war progressed. As Japanese troops were isolated by the Americans, the Japanese were forced to communicate code change instructions in the old system. We read these instructions and followed them. We had the information for the new codes at the same time as the Japanese troops. Two examples of prudence by the Americans were Rabaul and Bougainville. We could have forced the Japanese to surrender in these locations. Their isolation was a great source of information for us.

Despite these helpful hints from the Japanese, codebreaking was still a difficult process. Some analysts in the sorting room specialized in solving traffic that other analysts could not break out because of missing indicators or other garbles. Analysts were transferred to different units to lessen frustration. For a time, I served as a preliminary editor in the translators section. . .. I filled in check numbers, parentheses, and other routine information so that the translator could devote all of his time to the more difficult tasks of determining meaning. This experience helped our analytic work when we returned to cryptanalysis by enhancing our ability to recognize frequently used phrases. Our contribution to the war effort was very significant.

Chapter 4
Central Bureau: A Complete Signals Intelligence Agency

Deriving intelligence from an enemy's military communications is a complex process. Many disciplines are necessary to achieve the final result. These disciplines should not be considered in a vacuum; they are interdependent. Historians have concentrated on the achievements of cryptanalysts in World War II. These achievements are impressive and worthy of recognition. However, historians frequently misunderstand the complexities of cryptanalysis. Codebreaking would not be possible without the support of traffic analysis, clerical and machine support, translation, and information support services. As a complete signals intelligence agency, Central Bureau had not only traffic analysts and cryptanalysts but also a clerical and machine section, information support section, and linguists. The story of signals intelligence support to the Southwest Pacific theater would be incomplete without examining all of these additional fields that contributed to the mission.

The Trials and Tribulations of an IBM Operator

Sergeant (later Colonel) Donald Moreland was part of the second contingent of Americans who arrived in Australia in July 1942. He helped to establish the IBM section at Central Bureau and remained with that operation until the end of the war. His recollections attest to the ingenuity of Central Bureau participants in solving difficult problems.

I was a sophomore at North Carolina State University majoring in forestry when Uncle Sam found me. I was drafted into the Army in October 1941. After a quick course in teletype repair at Fort Monmouth, New Jersey, I was sent to the munitions building in Washington, D.C., in February 1942. At the munitions building, I learned how to install and repair the SIGABA. When I arrived in Melbourne, Australia, in the summer of 1942, my duties were to help set up MacArthur's message center. We faced several daunting challenges.

The message center was located in a former girls' school in Melbourne. My job was to set up the SIGABAs, but we had no tools or test meters. The only blueprints that we had were in our heads and what we could remember from our days at the munitions building. The lack of blueprints may have been because of security concerns. Fortunately, one of the members of our crew was an electrician. To test the electricity, he put a light bulb in an outlet, the bulb shorted, and he was almost knocked to the ground. That's when we found out that Australia did not have 110-volt current; Australia had 220-volt current. It was difficult to obtain the step-down transformers that we needed to make the SIGABA work. Step-down transformers had to be produced locally to get the quantity that we needed. This problem of incompatibility between machines and current stayed with us throughout the war.

When MacArthur's headquarters and Central Bureau moved to Brisbane, I left the SIGABA job and worked directly in Central Bureau. I was involved in setting up the IBM equip-

ment, which was a challenge, since I had never seen an IBM machine before. In the first shipment that we received, one box had a picture on it that was really helpful with the assembly of the machines. We had crate after crate of parts in numbered envelopes, but no parts list. Frazer, an American who was trained on the IBM machinery and part of the machine records unit, really saved us. He showed us what parts were for sorters, what parts were keypunches, etc.

For this time period, the IBM operation was quite sophisticated. After a message was punched up on the IBM cards, the cards were taken to the IBM room for sorting, collating, and printing. You could make the machines produce a variety of sorts, including both alphabetic and numeric printouts. An IBM machine read cards with a system of wire brushes that made contact with the slots in each card. Precise timing of machine parts was essential.

I thought we had it made when the second shipment of IBM equipment arrived at Central Bureau because these machines were 220-volt machines to match Australian current. However, we had a new set of problems. In those days, 220-volt motors from the U.S. had three phases. Now we had to contend with single-phase motors that required 110 volts of current and three-phase motors that required 220 volts of current. When we moved from Henry Street to the machine room at Ascot Park in late 1943, we had a transformer to step down each phase and then we had to balance the usage of

each phase. This problem stayed with us even when we moved to San Miguel, Luzon, the Philippines, in the spring and summer of 1945.

The engineering know-how at Central Bureau was quite remarkable. We kept the IBM machines going round-the-clock for almost four years. We could repair any part of the machine because we got wiring diagrams, contact sequences, and timing cycles. Because of this engineering know-how, we used the machines to do tasks that they were never designed to do. There was much creativity in our operation.

I enjoyed the working conditions at Central Bureau. Since most of the officers were not career officers and new to military life, things were very informal. Colonel Sinkov was more like a professor than a commander. It was a privilege to be invited to his home for supper. The only difference that I remember between officers and enlisted men was in the handling of mail. Outgoing mail was censored for enlisted personnel; officers' mail was not censored. During my time at Brisbane, I became an officer by direct commission. When I reported for work one afternoon, I was called up front and received my second lieutenant bars. Then I went to work as usual.

I supervised the swing shift in the IBM room for several years. Although all of the IBM operators were Americans, I enjoyed the contact with the Australians and other nationalities at Central Bureau. It was hard work; there were many sixteen-hour days. Leave was frequently cancelled *because of some emergency, but there was very little complaining at Central Bureau. We knew we had an important job to do and we did it to the best of our ability.*

When I returned home to Fort Devens, Massachusetts, in February 1946, the Army had one more surprise for me. As the sergeant was typing my separation papers, he asked me what my military occupational specialty [MOS] was. I did not have one because of the pressure of war. He looked at my experience and assigned me the MOS of machine records officer. Machine records was a critical skill. I had to stay in the Army until August 1946. After I left the Army, I obtained a Ph.D. in plant physiology and biochemistry. I remained in the reserves for thirty-two years. My experiences at Central Bureau were an extremely rewarding part of my career.

Supporting Central Bureau's Information Needs

Tristam Johnson was part of the first contingent of enlisted men to arrive in Australia directly from the U.S. He performed various information support functions for Central Bureau throughout the war. Johnson presents an interesting picture of various aspects of life at Central Bureau.

I was able to graduate from college in June 1941, because the draft law passed in 1940 exempted college seniors until after graduation. In the summer of 1941, I decided to enlist in the Army rather than wait for the draft, in order to have greater choice in my assignment. I had been involved with the theater in college so I arranged for Fort Monmouth [New Jersey] to request that I work on training films. Shortly after basic training, they asked for volunteers for the S15. It sounded interesting so I volunteered. I was sent to the munitions building in Washington, D.C., in February 1942. We worked on U.S. codes. When Singapore fell to the Japanese in February 1942, we were afraid that U.S. codes had been compromised. There was a great rush to create new codes. In April 1942, I was one of eight enlisted men sent to Melbourne, Australia. I remained at Central Bureau for the rest of the war. I performed numerous support tasks at Central Bureau. During the Melbourne period, I processed traffic and kept records of placenames and how these names were encoded. We regularly shared this information with Arlington Hall. Eventually, we started making our own maps because there were so few maps available. Those maps that were available lacked detailed information on the islands. As the war progressed, Central Bureau's information needs increased and mapmaking became our largest function. In late 1943, when we moved from Henry Street to Ascot Park in Brisbane, information support became a separate section, and I supervised about twelve people. I remember making a map to help locate the Yoshina Maru, the ship that sank in May 1944 off Aitape, New Guinea, from which we recovered an additive book.

The working atmosphere at Central Bureau was very friendly. When extra duties came along, we all willingly chipped in. For instance, when Central Bureau moved from Melbourne to Brisbane in September

1942, I was one of the equipment guards. We had to load and unload the equipment on several trains because each state in Australia has its own track gauge, which necessitated changing trains. The receipt of captured material was always a time of great excitement at Central Bureau. We all participated in the drying of the material captured at Sio, New Guinea. We needed every flat surface in Ascot Park to restore the pages of the code book from the Yoshino Maru.

Life in Australia was nice because the people were so hospitable. The Red Cross maintained lists of people who wanted soldiers to come to supper. We enjoyed many home-cooked meals. There was always room for one more soldier at an Australian dinner table. As one of the first Americans on the scene, I fully experienced Australian hospitality. During the early days, there were no barracks so we lived in Australian homes. The Australians appreciated our help.

There was one OCS for all of the services in Australia. In 1943, I was accepted for OCS training and became a second lieutenant. After returning to Central Bureau, I became a liaison officer, funneling information in and out of the Bureau. When Central Bureau moved to the Philippines in 1945, I went too. I worked in this same position, but we were stationed in Manila rather than in San Miguel, Luzon.

After the war, when I returned to civilian life, I embarked on a career in financial investments. I have fond memories of my Central Bureau experience.

A Central Bureau J-Boy

There is universal agreement on one point among students who study the Japanese language – it is very complex and difficult to learn. At the start of World War II, the U.S. military was hampered by a shortage of Japanese linguists. The need for Japanese linguists in the intelligence field was particularly acute. How did the Army recruit and train Japanese linguists? How were these new linguists able to meet the demands of translating intelligence quickly enough to be useful to the commanders? Robert C. Christopher's answers to these questions give an inkling of the challenges that faced linguists at Central Bureau. By the time Christopher arrived at Central Bureau in 1944, linguists were extremely busy because of the Sio capture. The Australian army's Ninth Infantry Division discovered the entire cryptographic library of the Japanese army's Twentieth Division at Sio, New Guinea, in January 1944.

Robert Christopher joined the Army in 1942. After attending language school and OCS, he served with the Signals Intelligence Service at Arlington Hall and at Central Bureau. After the war, Christopher obtained a bachelor's degree in

Robert C. Christopher

Japanese studies from Yale University. He was recalled to active duty during the Korean war and served as a senior Chinese linguist. Christopher pursued a career in journalism and held key editorial positions at both *Time* and *Newsweek* magazines. He is also the author of books on the Japanese culture and economy.

I became a J-boy, [the nickname for Japanese linguists in World War II] because my father suggested that I study Japanese. My father was a machine gunner in World War I. As my father put it: 'When we go to war with Japan, you will be better off as an intelligence officer than as a machine gunner'. In my freshman year at Yale University in September 1941, I began my studies of the Japanese language.

Shortly after Pearl Harbor, Verna Lorell came up to Yale from Washington, D.C., and talked to me about being a linguist in the Army. Since you could no longer volunteer, Lorell told me to inform him of my induction date and Arlington Hall would request me. The Army transferred me to Fort Devens, Massachusetts, and nobody sent for me. After being stuck on guard duty for a while, I contacted Lorell and eventually got to Arlington Hall.

The Japanese linguist school at Arlington Hall was superb. Edwin O. Reischauer ran the school, and all of the instructors were very good. It is interesting that there were no native Japanese instructors at Arlington Hall. Class size was small, only five or six people, and the instruction was intense. We learned classic or archaic Japanese, not conversational Japanese, because the Japanese mili-

tary sent messages in classic Japanese. The course lasted only a few months. Before we knew it, we were working in operations.

I was very impressed by my colleagues in the Japanese translation section at Arlington Hall. I was surrounded by extremely bright people from Harvard, Columbia, Princeton, and City College of New York. Our first activities in operations were to learn some cryptanalysis, stripping, and bookbreaking, so that we would have a better understanding of the context of our work.

We had been promised that we would receive OCS training after we completed language school. Because of operational necessity, we had OCS training half of the day and then spent the other half of the day at work. I was lucky to get my commission as a second lieutenant. One of my classmates, Joseph Kraft, who later became a well-known newspaper columnist, did not get his commission because he was only eighteen years old. I was nineteen. The Army went through the motions to try and make soldiers out of us by giving us physical training and conducting inspections, but they knew we were a lost cause. The military atmosphere at both Arlington Hall and Central Bureau was not very strict.

Since I wanted to go overseas, my stay at Arlington Hall was brief. I went to Central Bureau with eighteen to twenty other linguists in 1944. We didn't get any special briefing about Central Bureau before we left. Sinkov was already a legend at Arlington Hall. I knew he was at Central Bureau so I figured I would have an important job. I was relieved to finally make it to Brisbane. Our ship could not dock at Port Moresby as planned because the replacement depot was full. We ended up at Oro Bay, New Guinea. The colonel in charge tried to put us in the signal corps. I knew nothing about being a signals officer and was sure glad when Captain Howard W. Brown straightened things out [and] flew us to Brisbane.

At Central Bureau, I worked under Hugh Erskine, who ran the translation section. Erskine was the son of missionary parents and had a good command of the language because he had lived in Japan for many years. The best linguists at Central Bureau were Lieutenant Otto Mahrt and Captain Clarence Yamagata. Although he may have not had the official title, Otto Mahrt was the senior linguist. Otto was the final authority on language problems. The most helpful working aids that I had as a translator were those that Otto had developed. He interviewed prisoners of war and asked them how terms were used and then passed the information to all of the translators. The second linguist of note, Clarence Yamagata, spoke and wrote Japanese fluently. Clarence was nisei [second-generation Japanese] from Hawaii. Clarence was most helpful explaining Japanese usage, which was invaluable when dealing with such a complex language. Because of his difficulties with English, Clarence was not as fluent with translation. There were no restrictions on his access to information because of being nisei. Clarence Yamagata was so highly regarded by his colleagues

that they dedicated the Signals Intelligence Service Record to him. [The Signals Intelligence Service Record was the unclassified history written by Central Bureau participants in the fall of 1945.]

I supervised a team of five linguists. These various teams that I supervised were made up of Americans, British, and Australians. I was very impressed with the interallied aspects of Central Bureau. There were no international tensions. We were integrated very well. Jobs were assigned by talent. For instance, an Australian supervised the team next to mine. It was a very efficient operation.

Most of the messages that we translated dealt with ship movements or troop movements. There are a few out of the ordinary messages that still stand out in my memory. One translation was about the promotion of Japanese officers. It was boring until I learned that one man was promoted for breaking a U.S. Air Force code. This information was quickly passed to the appropriate channels. Another time, I was struggling with some words that meant Faerey [name of manufacturer] Fireflies. I could not imagine that the Japanese would send messages about Fireflies. I checked my work and did not see any mistakes. After talking to my colleagues, I learned that a Firefly is a British naval plane. The British had just sent a detachment to the Pacific, so my message was really about Fireflies; a British carrier had five Fireflies on board. The most thrilling translation that I worked on was a message that came in the clear when I was the senior linguist at San Miguel,

Luzon. We knew the message had to be important because it was sent in the clear. It contained words that I had never seen before. For instance, the word Chin. Eventually I found the right dictionary and discovered that Chin stood for I. The only person allowed to use this particular expression was the emperor of Japan. I was translating Emperor Hirohito's 14 August message telling the troops to surrender.

In the spring of 1945, when I had moved up to San Miguel, I was astonished to receive a letter from Yale University asking if I was coming back to school since the war was winding down. I was scheduled to go with the troops as an interpreter in operations Olympic and Coronet to invade Japan. I was worried about being dead, never mind going back to school. I was relieved when the U.S. dropped the atomic bomb and Japan surrendered.

After the war, I was a member of the Target Intelligence Committee [TICOM] team that went to Japan to learn about the Japanese cryptographic capabilities. We were briefed on our mission by Rufus Taylor, a naval officer. The briefing was very general and no specific targets were given to us. We had a carte blanche letter from General Eikleberger stating that we could go anywhere or do anything necessary to fulfill our mission. The letter even stated that local commanders should give us combat troop support if we requested it. My partner Sid Haken and I went to the Japanese signal corps headquarters, the equivalent of our headquarters at Fort Monmouth. We found many copies of The Black Chamber by Yardley, which had been translated into Japanese. All of the code books and other equipment were gone. Even the personnel were gone. We did not gain any useful knowledge from this effort. I came back to the U.S. and got out of the Army in July 1946. As I think back on my Central Bureau experience, I am amazed that we were able to do such an effective job in light of our limited training.

A Bizarre Experiment

It is interesting to examine the contrasting experiences of Curtis Nelson and Robert Christopher. Although both worked as linguists, their opportunities for training were very different. Curtis Nelson's experiences illustrate some of the training and planning difficulties the military had in meeting the Japanese challenge.

Curtis H. Nelson was a native of Minneapolis, Minnesota. In preparation for a career in court reporting and convention reporting, Nelson studied stenography operations at the University of Minnesota. He was inducted into the Army in September 1942.

Curtis H. Nelson

During my first year in the military, I did office work handling the papers of new recruits. I was stationed at Fort Snelling, Minnesota. In the fall of 1943, the Army summoned all personnel with stenotyping skills to Pittsburg, California, to participate in an experimental program. There were a total of ten of us with these skills. We flew to Brisbane, Australia, and were assigned to the 126th SRI Company. Our job was to monitor Japanese broadcasts and record what we heard on our stenograph machines. Since information is recorded phonetically on stenograph machines and I had no knowledge of Japanese, this task was extremely difficult. After five months of this monitoring, I was sent to Central Bureau. Of the ten stenotypists, I was the only one sent to Central Bureau. My colleagues did not have the background or stamina to continue this experiment.

At Central Bureau they gave me a Japanese dictionary and told me to learn the language. Each day, Clarence Yamagata dictated Japanese to me and I would type the Japanese into English. I worked up to 100 Japanese words a minute, but I was very frustrated. Finally I asked to see Colonel Doud. [Colonel Doud was the American assistant director of Central Bureau for a brief period before Colonel Sinkov assumed this duty.]

I wanted to find out why I was learning to copy Japanese on a stenograph machine. After I learned enough Japanese, G-2 was planning to send me beyond the Japanese front lines to tap phones and copy what I heard on the stenographic machine. Runners would then take the tapes back to headquarters for translation. I immediately lost my interest in learning any more Japanese. I would last about three minutes if I went beyond the Japanese front line. With my help, the Army abandoned this experiment.

Next, I was assigned as a scanner in the translation section under Colonel Erskine. I circled key words on IBM printouts and then turned the printouts over to the translators. We looked for such words as Maru [ship] and placename locations. This work was much more satisfying because I saw ships and locations and then later saw that such-and-such ship sank. It is unfortunate that intercept operators were not told more about how they fit into the total picture and what they accomplished. These operators would have had greater job satisfaction if they [had known] the importance of their work.

I enjoyed my stay at Central Bureau. I especially liked working with people from so many different countries. I also liked living as a civilian even though I was in the military. I had an apartment in town and did not have to live in the barracks. I was also able to play in a band at night.

I left for home on 31 December 1945. The Army's lack of planning and lack of training remain a mystery to me.

Linguists played an important role at CBB. (Source S.I.S. Record)

FRONT ROW: Harrison Pearce, James Walter, Otto Mahrt, Hugh S. Erskine, Stuart Johnson, Clarence Yamagata, Sidney Doggett, Robert Christopher
SECOND ROW: Andrew Wiedman, Leonard Martin, H. Hourne, B. Polack, C. Carrington, W. Kalbfell, C. Archer
THIRD ROW: Eugene Aleinkoff, W. Wilkes, R. Lawrence, J. Smart, G. Howard

Chapter 5
The Role of Women at Central Bureau

Women played an important role in the success of Central Bureau. One measure of the importance of women is General Akin's attempt to obtain an exemption from the Australian government to permit Australian women to move to the Philippines with the rest of Central Bureau in 1945. Australian law forbade the use of women in overseas duty, however, and General Akin's plea for an exemption was denied.

Women served at all of Central Bureau's locations. Australian and American women were located at Melbourne, Brisbane, and field sections in Australia; only American women served at San Miguel, Luzon, in the Philippines and in New Guinea. The majority of women were keypunch operators, typists, and intercept operators. Women belonged to units of the Australian Women's Auxiliary Service (AWAS), the Women's Australian Auxiliary Air Force (WAAAF), or the U.S. Women's Army Corp (WAC). Australian women were involved in SIGINT from the beginning of Central Bureau. The WACs came later in the war.

The following description of life as an intercept operator, by Joy Linnane, a member of the WAAAF, demonstrates some of the difficulties intercept operators faced whether they were men or women. She was one of thirteen women to complete the first WAAAF Kana class on 6 July 1942. Ms. Linnane served at Point Cook, located just outside Melbourne, Australia, at an RAAF station in 1942 when few intercept units were in the field. This account was taken from *The Eavesdroppers* by Jack Bleakley.

At Point Cook, we quickly learned the price of working for an intelligence unit – it was isolation. We were bar-racked apart from everyone in an old house formerly used as married quarters. The hut where we worked was near the SIGS school and was known as the 'hush-hush' hut. I soon learned that all of the SIGS were instructed not to approach us. Since we worked Tokyo time, we were out of step with the rest of the station. During my six-month tour, I never ate in the mess. We collected what food was available and cooked it ourselves over a radiator in the hut.

We worked four hours on and four hours off, intercepting Japanese navy messages passed on to an unknown person or persons. Rarely did we ever have more than two hours of sleep at one time. We had a brief course in unarmed defense and in the use of firearms. We worked behind bolted doors and shaded windows. A Smith & Wesson revolver was always kept at the door and there was an emergency button near each AR7, the radio sets we used. It was a memorable experience.

The Army was the only section of the U.S. military that permitted women to take overseas duty. WACs served in every theater of World War II. Having women in the military was a new experience for the services. How did the Army treat the WACs who served with Central Bureau? The following perspectives from a WAC in Brisbane, the WACs in New Guinea, and the commanding officers of the New Guinea unit provide interesting answers to this question.

The Brisbane Perspective

Sally Speer joined the WACs in 1943. When offered the choice of going to OCS or overseas, Sally chose overseas. She arrived in Brisbane in September 1944. She moved forward to San Miguel, Luzon, the Philippines, on 1 August 1945 as part of the relocation of most of Central Bureau to a location closer to MacArthur's general headquarters.

I enjoyed my experience at Central Bureau immensely. I especially enjoyed the opportunity to meet and work with so many interesting people. As a keypunch operator for the machine unit, there was plenty to do. For most of my tour, I had the graveyard or midnight shift of duty. People assume that the keypunching equipment was IBM because the sorters and tabulators were IBM. However, the keypunching equipment was really Remington Rand. The military did not tap my talents and abilities. Before my military service, I was a secretary for the president of a large corporation in New York City. Keypunching was not challenging enough for me, but it was essential for our mission.

I was glad to be in Brisbane rather than in New Guinea. We had more freedom to move about in the city. In New Guinea, WACs could not go anywhere unless they were accompanied by a G.I. because we were close to the war front. The climate in Brisbane was certainly better than the climate in New Guinea. Although the hours were long and leave was frequently cancelled, I was glad to have the opportunity to serve overseas and to do my part in bringing about victory.

The New Guinea Perspective

From April 1944 onward, the pace of war in the Southwest Pacific theater increased rapidly. The Allied strategy of bypassing Japanese strongholds to attack in unexpected areas where the Japanese had fewer forces was very effective. MacArthur's island-hopping campaign through New Guinea isolated many Japanese units as he raced to the Philippines. The invasion of the Philippines began with the capture of Leyte. The invasion, originally planned for December 1944, was moved up to October. The Japanese were tenacious fighters, and the war was far from over. Personnel to collect SIGINT were in demand; WACs were sent to the Southwest Pacific theater to meet this demand.

The following information is based on recollections by Susan Cross Santa Maria, Maryjane Ford Walter, and Phyllis Purse, three WACs who served in the cryptographic unit at Hollandia, New Guinea. Their background and training varied. Before enlisting in the WACs, Susan was a laboratory tech-

First WACs to come to Brisbane made their home at Yeronga. (Source: S.I.S. Record)

American and Dutch WACs joined in standing retreat at Yeronga. (Source: S.I.S. Record)

nician at Jefferson Hospital in Philadelphia. After basic training, she served at a hospital in Long Island, New York. Maryjane had two years of college and one year of business school prior to her enlistment in the WACs. After basic training, she was a code clerk at Fort McClure, Wisconsin. She was the first WAC to receive the Soldiers' Medal, which was presented to her for her courage in saving a G.I. from drowning. Both Susan and Maryjane were members of the WAC cryptographic training class conducted at Vint Hill, Virginia.

At MacArthur's suggestion, a special class for WACs was set up at Vint Hill, Virginia. Two women from each of the nine WAC commands were selected for this training.

Phyllis Purse was a secretary in a paper company prior to her enlistment in the Women's Auxiliary Army Corps in 1942. The Women's Auxiliary Army Corps was reorganized and became the WAC in the summer of 1943. Phyllis served at Daytona Beach, Florida, and at Fort Sill, Oklahoma, where she drove trucks to various message centers. She had three' weeks of keypunch training before she went overseas. These women give the reader a glimpse of the logistical problems that the Army had in general as well as specific

logistical problems for WACs. The information in the following oral history was taken from a joint interview of all three ladies.

Life in the Army was full of surprises. Members of the Vint Hill cryptographic class were promised that they would become tech sergeants when they graduated, but it never happened. Although twenty WACs graduated from the class, only nineteen went overseas. The twentieth graduate was already a tech sergeant. She could not go overseas because she had no company to command. Officers had to have a company to be eligible for overseas duty. We learned to expect the unexpected.

When we went to sleep aboard ship on 23 October 1944, we were 200 miles from Brisbane, Australia. When we woke up the next morning, we were no longer going southwest, but were going north to New Guinea. The Leyte invasion was under way. The ship stopped at Milne Bay [New Guinea] to take on more troops. Some of the WACs, including Susan, were taken off the ship at Oro Bay to make room for more combat troops. The WACs finally ended up in Hollandia. There was much confusion when we arrived at Hollandia because our orders were still at Brisbane. We were taken to Imbi Bay [Hollandia, New Guinea]. After six weeks, we were finally taken back to Sentani Lake [Hollandia], where we originally landed, to begin our cryptographic work.

Our work on Japanese shipping was very interesting. Japan divided the territory that it controlled into five areas. *Every ship had to report to its area each day. In turn, each area had to report to Tokyo each day. We were gratified when we received a code book that was captured near Truk [Dublon Island]. We saw that we had recovered 96 percent of the additive by ourselves and had few mistakes. Our unit received a letter of commendation from Colonel Sinkov for this.*

Life was rugged in both New Guinea and the Philippines. We flew to San Miguel, Luzon, the Philippines, in June 1945. Our barracks were in a rice paddy. The huts where we lived and worked had wooden floors, tin roofs, and burlap sides with openings above the floor and below the roof. It was so hot that we could not work in the huts from noon to 3:00 P.M. When the typhoon season started, we were even warmer because the side openings had to be covered with corrugat-

ed tin. The soldiers and sailors who served in the area with us were very generous and made life bearable for us. We were especially lucky in Hollandia because the Seventh Naval Fleet had a recreation area right in back of our base. We also went out of the way to help the men. We visited the wounded. Unlike the nurses, who were extremely busy, we could take the time to comb their hair and make them feel comfortable. Unfortunately, the general public viewed WACs, especially those who went overseas, as men-chasers. We did not deserve this reputation. The Army should have made greater efforts to correct this misconception.

Our voyages to and from the Southwest Pacific area sure were memorable. There were 5,000 troops on the ship. We got two meals a day. We snuck on deck whenever we could,

The WACs who ended up at Setani Lake, Hollandia, instead of Brisbane
waited at Imbi Bay for their orders to arrive.

especially to sleep, because it was very hot. Nine of us were in a cabin for two. The room was so small that we had to schedule when we got dressed. Each tier would take a turn getting up first. We had one helmet full of fresh water per person per day. Sometimes we used it to wash clothes. There was one bathtub for thirty-two people in a congregate of cabins. Sometimes we would pool all of the water, fill the tub, and take turns taking a bath. You had to wear fatigues on the ship, but they gave us only one pair. WACs were not allowed to go on 'A' promenade deck in anything but pants. The reason you could not wear a skirt was because the men were lying and sitting in various forms on 'A' deck. Once you washed your fatigues in the salt water, it took them thirty-six hours to dry. When you couldn't wear your fatigues, you wore your class A uniform, which was a skirt and blouse, so you had to stay below deck. We were at sea for twenty-six days so it was wonderful to get off that ship.*

A View from the Commanders

Lieutenant Victor Rose was the commanding officer, and Lieutenant John R. Thomas was operations officer for the detachment of WACs who served in Hollandia in late 1944. Victor Rose was drafted in 1941. Prior to that, he was an accountant. His cryptologic training at Fort Monmouth, New Jersey, was cut short because of manpower needs. He went to the munitions building in Washington, D.C., early in 1942. All of his experience at both the munitions building and Arlington Hall was in the cryptologic section. Rose went to OCS in 1943. He arrived at Central Bureau Brisbane in May 1944, and in 1945 he went to Hollandia to command the WAC unit. John Thomas, who was drafted shortly after the Japanese attacked Pearl Harbor, was assigned to the Signal Corps at Camp Crowder, Missouri, and became a radio operator. In February 1943, Thomas attended OCS at Fort Monmouth and also went to signals and message center training. After a brief tour at Arlington Hall, Thomas was sent to Central Bureau Brisbane. In January 1945, Thomas went to Hollandia to work with the WAC unit.

It is significant that the WAC unit had cryptanalytic tasks because it gives some indication that women were not relegated only to stereotypic jobs. However, it is also interesting to note that the commanders of this unit were men. When the unit

Victor Rose

John R. Thomas

moved to San Miguel, Luzon, the Philippines, in June 1945, Rose and Thomas were assigned to other duties, such as planning for the invasion of Japan, and lost track of the unit. When the war ended, they were part of the TICOM operation that looked for cryptographic information in Japan. They left military service early in 1946. The information in this oral history came from a joint interview with both men.

Commanding a unit of WACs was an interesting experience. There were 350 women in the unit. We were our own separate B branch, so the women had little contact with other Americans in Hollandia. As a cryptographic unit, we worked primarily on the Japanese Army Water Transport Code. Our traffic was dated, but our work was important because we filled in the gaps. We had to fill in code books without the assistance of IBM equipment. The traffic was delivered by courier, and it came either from Brisbane or directly from the site. We were under Central Bureau control so we had no reason to communicate with Arlington Hall.

We carefully maintained security. A guard was posted outside the hut where we worked at all times. We burned our trash every day, which simplified our move to the Philippines in 1945. Outgoing personal mail was censored. One of the recruits wrote in Polish. Since neither of us knew Polish, we had to send this correspondence to another base for censorship.

The best way to achieve productivity was by permitting flexibility. Since the heat in the hut where we worked was unbearable, we gave each person a quota of messages to complete each day. Once the quotas were met, they

were free for the remainder of the day. Some finished their work quickly while others struggled along all day. Another challenge that we faced was that the WACs came to Hollandia with different amounts of training, from cryptographic training at Vint Hill to no training at all. We had to do some teaching ourselves and if someone did not catch on, we had to find something that they could do. Although we asked to be reassigned to other duties when the unit moved to the Philippines, our time with the WACs was rewarding.

Chapter 6
The FRUMEL Experience

When considering SIGINT support to the Southwest Pacific theater, the story would be incomplete without looking at the participation of Fleet Radio Unit Melbourne (FRUMEL). In February 1942, the U.S. Navy joined a small signals intelligence unit from the Royal Australian Navy (RAN) to form the joint military organization FRUMEL. FRUMEL's contributions to the war effort are impressive especially because it was a small signals intelligence unit: there were only a few hundred personnel at FRUMEL and its forward units. At the end of the war, the U.S. Navy had 775 receivers in the Pacific theaters, and only 58 of these receivers were in Australia. Allied victories that occurred in part because of the invaluable intelligence provided by FRUMEL include the Battle of Midway in 1942 and the captures of Lae, New Guinea, in 1943 and Biak, New Guinea, in 1944, which helped MacArthur advance through New Guinea to the Philippines. FRUMEL directly distributed its communications intelligence to the commander of the Seventh Fleet, to the commander of the Southwest Pacific theater, General Douglas MacArthur, and to the submarine command in western Australia.

Although FRUMEL was a joint military organization of U.S. and Australian personnel, each had its own administration covering personnel, supplies, etc. Each navy maintained its own communications, had separate code rooms, and handled reporting functions separately. The important traffic analysis, cryptanalysis, and language sections were operated jointly. There was excellent cooperation between the two navies, and the organization ran smoothly.

In January 1945, the Americans turned FRUMEL facilities over to the Australians. A small nucleus of Americans remained in Melbourne until the end of the war. The U.S. took this action because the war front was now a considerable distance north of Australia. OP-20-G had centralized processing so it was not as dependent on field processing as it had been earlier in the war. Melbourne continued to provide communications intelligence to the RAN until the end of the war.

The participants at FRUMEL tell their stories on the following pages. The intercept operators, traffic analysts, cryptanalysts, machine personnel, and linguists were the lifeblood of FRUMEL as they are in any communications intelligence organization. They present a vivid picture of their challenges and contributions.

From the Ground Up at FRUMEL

James B. Capron joined the Navy in 1936. From 1936 to 1940, Capron was a radioman on various ships. Capron was a member of the last "on the roof gang" (OTRG) class, which intercepted Japanese codes. The class had this title because the Navy actually conducted classes on Japanese intercept on the top of its building on Constitution Avenue in Washington, D.C. Because of a leaky roof and other poor conditions, Capron's class could not be completed and they moved to OP-20-G office spaces. They held class in the evenings when the offices were not in use. Capron was an intercept operator in Hawaii and on Corregidor. Capron's story of reaching Melbourne by way of Java is most interesting. His involvement in FRUMEL from the beginning offers an important perspective.

On 5 February 1942, I left Corregidor bound for Java. We were the first naval group to leave Corregidor. It was not an evacuation. We were assigned to support the Dutch in Java because of a recent alliance between the U.S. and the Netherlands. We got James B. Capron, Jr. off to an inauspicious start.

We could not tell anyone that we were leaving, and we could not take anything but the clothes on our backs. We made our own boxes for the typewriters, receivers, and other equipment. We even took a portable direction finding set with us that we never had a chance to use. We had five minutes to get aboard the submarine because they did not want to stay on the surface too long as the Japanese were in the area. We had so much trouble getting the direction finding set on board because of its size. They had to open a torpedo chute to get the tripod portion on the sub. It was so crowded on the ship that we had to walk on cases of supplies to get around. Although the submarine had many bullet holes, it was operative and we made it to Java.

James B. Capron, Jr.

Our mission on Java was the same as it had been on Corregidor. We intercepted Japanese traffic, but now we warned the Dutch of impending enemy attacks. We set up shop in converted stables in Bandung, Java. We had three shifts with two people on each watch. The mission was short-lived, however, as the Japanese landed on Java three weeks after our arrival. The Japanese landed on the northern part of the island at 2200 hours, and we were evacuated by 0630 the following morning. We spent the night riding on a bus. We had to travel over 110 miles from Bandung to Tjilatjap, a port on the southern coast of Java [now known as Cilacap]. I was in the shower when the word came to board the submarine. I didn't even have time to rinse off. The sub started moving so I had to leap on board.

We arrived at Exmouth, Australia. Swede Carlson was in charge of our group. He had to commandeer seats on trains to get us to Melbourne. We made the trip, not as a unit, but three or four at a time depending on how many seats were available. We were involved in FRUMEL from the ground up. When we arrived in the beginning of March 1942, the intercept station was still under construction.

The intercept site was at Moorabbin, a suburb of Melbourne. We pitched in to help the Australians build the station because progress was slow. There was a shortage of Australian manpower because its navy was small and all of the younger men were on sea duty. In short order, we converted a farm into a first-rate intercept station. There were two houses on the premises. The first was reserved for the chief's quarters. The second house was reserved for the Australian women in the RAAN. We converted a shack into office work space. We strung poles for the antenna[s] and built a barracks for the enlisted men. When the first group of evacuees from Corregidor arrived, they helped us complete our work.

The analytic section for FRUMEL was in Melbourne at the Monterey Apartments. We used half of the apartment building; Australian civilians were tenants in the rest of the building. Australian couriers delivered traffic from Moorabbin by motorcycle every two hours.

We worked side by side with the Australian naval personnel. I enjoyed them very much. Ninety percent of the Australian staff were women. I taught them to use the typewriter instead of copying code by hand. They learned quickly and were excellent operators.

Our mission at FRUMEL was similar to our mission at Corregidor – intercept Japanese traffic and get the information out. We sent bearings directly to the Seventh Fleet. We had no mechanism to send raw traffic electrically to Washington. Later on in the war, we started providing detachments to work on ships. I was part of the detachment that provided direct support for the Leyte invasion in October 1944.

Two teams from FRUMEL were established to support the Leyte invasion, which was the first step in reconquering the Philippines. My team was supposed to go on the ship named the Princeton. We flew from Brisbane to Hollandia, New Guinea, where we learned that the Princeton had already left for duty. This was a fortunate break for me because it later sank. We were assigned to the Wassach Liberty ship under Commander Baird. Our mission was protection of the ship, not strategic planning for the invasion. We were assigned to transmitter room three. Since army communications domi-

The intercept site at Bandung, Java, was short-lived because of the advancing Japanese. They fled Java to Australia via the port of Cilacap.

nated the ship, we had trouble getting antennas. The army personnel were always telling us when to connect and disconnect. The invasion battle was very fierce. Our ship was very close to the shore. I saw MacArthur go ashore for a staged photo opportunity. Our nickname for MacArthur was "Dugout Doug."

I returned to the U.S. in November 1944. I believe that FRUMEL closed by the end of the year and that Australia took over the facilities at Melbourne. I left the Navy in 1956 and joined NSA as a civilian. I retired from NSA in December 1971. Our contributions to the war effort at FRUMEL were significant. I was glad to be a part of the unit.

Intercept and Traffic Analysis at FRUMEL

The major source of intercept for FRUMEL was at Moorabbin, a suburb of Melbourne. The Navy also had forward intercept units in Townsville, which is located in Queensland, Adelaide River, which is located in the Northern Territory, and Exmouth Gulf in western Australia. The Townsville unit was operational for about a year. The unit at Adelaide River was the most successful. It lasted for the duration of the war. This unit had a permanent circuit to Fleet Radio Unit Pacific (FRUPAC) and moved forward with Admiral Nimitz's headquarters in 1945. The unit at Exmouth Gulf had direction finding responsibilities but was plagued by equipment problems. The Navy also attempted to set up a forward unit at Cooktown, which is along the northern coast of Australia in Queensland. The Navy established Cooktown in February 1944 but did not have the resources to make the station successful, and it was decommissioned in October 1944.

The pace of the war quickened dramatically in 1944, with MacArthur's leap to Hollandia, New Guinea, in April and the invasion of Leyte in October 1944. In light of these events, the lack of resources for Cooktown is understandable. The fol-

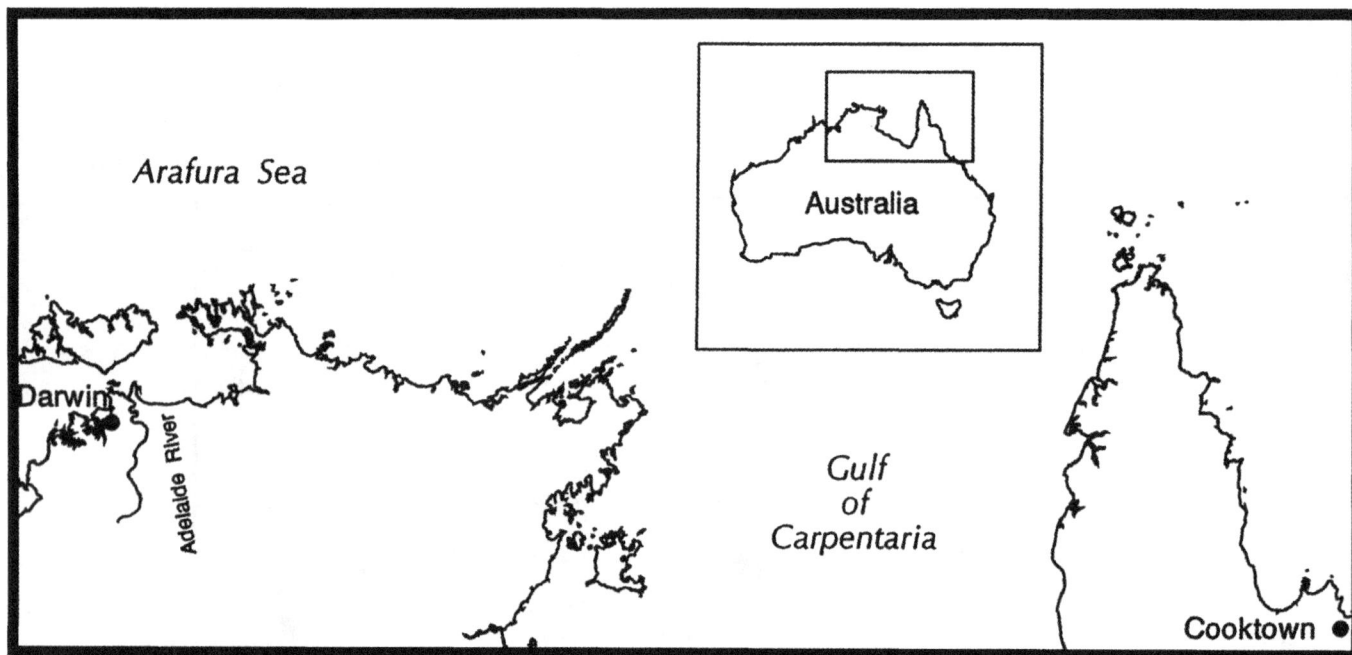

The Adelaide River was the location of a successful forward intercept site operated by FRUMEL. FRUMEL was unable to maintain its intercept site at Cooktown. Its remote location made the delivery of supplies extremely difficult.

The headquarters of FRUMEL was located in the residential section of Melbourne. It received intercept from Moorabbin, a suburb of Melbourne.

lowing excerpts attest to the versatility and talent of the navy SIGINT personnel.

A Conversation with the Operators

(Note: In addition to individual oral history interviews, information was obtained from "Japanese Intercept Down Under, Part II, Adelaide River," by Sid Burnett, *NCVA Cryptolog*, Summer 1984.)

The following recollections from Chief Warrant Officers Sidney Burnett, John H. Gelineau, and David W. Snyder portray the everyday activities involved in the collection and analysis of traffic. They performed the bread-and-butter basic tasks of a communications intelligence organization. Their backgrounds and experiences are similar. All started out in the Navy as radiomen, and all attended various OTRG ("On the Roof Gang") classes.

Sidney A. Burnett

John H. Gelineau

Burnett joined the Navy in 1927 and was selected for special training in the eighth OTRG class in April 1932. Gelineau joined the Navy in 1929. He was a member of the tenth OTRG class, which graduated in 1934. Snyder joined the Navy in the mid-1930s. Because the depression created a flood of applications, Snyder was on a waiting list for a year and a half before he was accepted into the Navy. Snyder attended the twenty-second OTRG class in 1938. At the time of Pearl Harbor and the U.S. entrance into World War II, all were stationed in the Philippines at Corregidor. All were evacuated from Corregidor and then went to Melbourne to join FRUMEL. Snyder was part of the first group that left Corregidor, did a short stint in Java, and then came to Melbourne. Burnett and Gelineau were part of the last group that was evacuated from Corregidor. Here is their story.

Burnett: We received excellent training on how to intercept Japanese traffic in the OTRG class. We really did have class in a room on the roof of that building on Constitution Avenue. It was a concrete block. Perhaps it was intended to be an elevator room. The Navy was very concerned about security so we all had to wear civilian clothes. When I got to Washington, all I had were uniforms. Dick Long sent me to a nearby tailor named Rosenthal. I bet the Navy gave him lots of business.

Snyder: You are right. Security was very strict. The guards knew us by sight so we did not have a badge system. The eight students and our instructor were in a room approximately twelve-by-twenty feet. Some of the requirements for the OTRG were to be single, a second or third class radioman, and have thirty months of active duty remaining after graduation. I had to reenlist to keep this assignment.

Burnett: My instructor, Malcolm Lamb, told us to think of ourselves as Japanese operators and to take on their philosophy so that we could understand and remember their radio procedures.

Gelineau: The first thing we learned was how to copy the Hiragana [phonetic alphabet of forty-six characters] characters in longhand. I was so glad that I always had a typewriter in the field and did not have to copy these characters. After completing Hiragana, we copied code by typing on the RIPS typewriters. The RIPS was a modified Underwood typewriter with extra keys so that you could type both Katakana characters and English characters. We also had an intelligence publication that gave formats for copying different types of messages. I did not learn about OP-20-G until I completed the class.

Snyder: My experience in the OTRG was different because we had work assignments in addition to our studies. During the early part of the class, we also did keypunch work in the Navy Department. Toward the end of the class, we actually spent some of the day working at the intercept station at Cheltenham, Maryland. It was good preparation for our wartime duties.

Snyder: I am sure that we all agree that it was wonderful to finally get to Melbourne. The Monterey Apartments, where FRUMEL offices were housed, were brand new when I came to Melbourne early in March 1942. They remind me of today's garden apartments. I spent my time at Moorabbin, the intercept station out-

side of Melbourne. The RAANs who worked with us were using a different system called Tiddley to copy traffic. Tiddley was a system that used the Roman alphabet when possible. When you needed a combination that was not available, such as YU, you wrote a y and overscored it. The RAANs did everything by hand and did not know the Romaji character system. Our first task was to teach them our system. They learned quickly and did not object to using the typewriter. The RAANs were excellent workers. They did not seek special privileges. They worked right alongside us doing the same manual tasks that we did. The Japanese encrypted their callsigns by using a substitution system. We were generally able to recover the callsigns. This was the first task of the night shift because everything else depended on getting the right callsigns. The most frustrating and challenging callsign for us to break was a general navy callsign used on ships. Sometimes knowing the shore station helped us know which ship the message was from. We never did break that general navy callsign. Moorabbin was the staging area for sending men to Adelaide River, Northern Territory. Adelaide River was closer to the operations so I was dying to go there. There was a direct landline from Adelaide River to our offices in Melbourne. The teletype machines at FRUMEL headquarters ran twenty-four hours a day to accept the flow of traffic from Adelaide River.

Burnett: I was involved in building the Adelaide River station. After the Navy decided to locate a new intercept station as far north as possible,

LTJG Keith (Keg) Goodwin and I headed north to get the job done. We made our selection on 28 January 1943, and by the end of March we were operational. We set up shop on the old Marakai Ranch property just east of the center of the river. The RAAF helped us put that station together. We could not build any buildings because we did not want to attract Japanese attention. We worked out of eight-man tents that we borrowed from the nearby Australian army camp. What a mess, especially in the rainy season. The fellow who operated the teletype machine to Melbourne had to keep his feet on the table to avoid getting a shock each time he hit a key.

Snyder: I never did get transferred to Adelaide River.

Gelineau: I worked at the Monterey Apartments. I kept trying to get out to Moorabbin, but I never did. I worked in the traffic analysis section as a statistician. I filed messages by callsign, point of origin, etc. There was a constant flow of information between Washington, Hawaii, and FRUMEL in support of traffic analysis. Each day, each center sent out a technical report on traffic that kept all of us on our toes. Text messages that would assist us in traffic analysis were always made available to us.

Burnett: I was lucky. I had a wide variety of tasks at FRUMEL. My first task was to put my old DT together. This piece of equipment was taken from Corregidor to Java and then to Melbourne by the first group that left Corregidor. I was the direction-finding man on Corregidor and had operated that piece of equipment. The DT is a so-called walk-around high-frequency direction finder. It is actually an antenna that revolves around a receiver. I helped to develop this equipment under Commander Safford back in 1937.

Snyder: There were only direction finding training activities at Moorabbin. We received information from the British worldwide direction finding nets.

Burnett: After I made the DT operational and it was shipped to Exmouth Gulf, I spent my time trying to establish forward intercept units. Adelaide River and Townsville were very successful, but Cooktown was another story. The major problems at Cooktown were getting enough people and equipment to do the work. Plans for the intercept site at Cooktown began in July 1943. We finally got some personnel for Cooktown in February 1944. We got receivers from the RAAF and a broken generator from Melbourne. Cooktown was a washout because we ran out of food and water. We could not get a tank to pump water in, and the ships were too busy moving and supporting MacArthur. We did the best we could, but the resources just were not there.

Snyder: We all left Melbourne around the same time in the fall of 1944. After FRUMEL, I went to Kunming, China. I had various intercept assignments there. I went back to the States in February 1946. My contribution to the war effort was my long hours of intercept. I put the signals down on paper as perfectly as possible. I always strove to get every signal and not to miss even one.

Gelineau: After Melbourne, I went back to Hawaii. I really liked it there because I got to be the materials officer, which is something that I [had] always wanted to do. As the materials officer, I had to keep the traffic flowing and the equipment running. General navy communications was also located at this intercept site. It was difficult to keep the lines open to Washington because general communications did not know what we in the intelligence section did. My wartime experience was very rewarding.

Burnett: After Melbourne, I went back to the States. I was stationed in San Francisco as the fleet photographic officer. The Navy felt that they needed more publicity on the war in the Pacific. I was to set up communications so that we could get pictures from the war front and then get these pictures in the papers. The most memorable picture that we obtained was that of the marines running up the flag at Iwo Jima. This is the same picture that now appears in history books. I was glad to play a part in our victory over Japan.

Life at a Forward Unit

(The following excerpt, entitled 'Potshot 1943,' by Gordon I. Bower, was taken from "Japanese Intercept Down Under, Part II," *NCVA Cryptolog,* Summer 1984.)

In the spring of 1943, I and two other white hats, Charles A. Ross and Keith W. Smith, plus RMC Charles F. Jarrett, were informed that we were going to Base Potshot at Exmouth

Gulf. Potshot was a small naval advanced supply and refueling base, which was activated to provide topping off services to the submarines operating out of Perth, Australia.

Upon arriving at Exmouth Gulf, we became instant Seabees [members of a construction battalion]. The commanding officer at the base could not spare any manpower to help us set up the station. He gave us a bulldozer, a grader, and a Quonset hut, and told us to go to it. We cleared an area in the bush about a half mile from the base perimeter and became operational.

The first mistake that we made was to rely on the nearby Australian army unit, which assured us that they could give us an accurate position. Shortly thereafter, we received a marvelously succinct message from FRUMEL signed by John M. Lietwiler. 'Your reported position is eight miles out in the gulf. Since the buoyancy of your equipment is highly doubtful, recompute and provide accurate position soonest'.

Our mission was to provide line bearings on unidentified enemy callsigns. We produced a daily summary that was encrypted manually in a cumbersome British system and hand carried to the nearby Australian army unit. The Australian army unit transmitted the information to FRUMEL for us.

My special memories at Exmouth Gulf include the ankle-deep dust during the dry season and the incredible bogs when it rained. Staying awake during the night shift was never a

problem. There were frequent rumors of enemy commando landings, which were kept alive by the kangaroos that congregated around the DT and coughed like men. We always panicked on the first sound of a transmitter tuning up with V's out in the bush and were relieved to determine that the source of the sound was really one of the many unique birds or other critters in the area. We were the only troops allowed outside the base perimeter after dark. Luckily, our crew was relieved in six months. Our station closed within the year because the battle arena moved north.

Two Views of Cryptanalysis at FRUMEL

The Challenges of Cryptanalysis

John E. (Vince) Chamberlin joined the Navy in 1929. After several years at sea as a yeoman, Chamberlin was sent to Washington, D.C., in July 1939 to work in the radio central communications division. He learned cryptanalysis and volunteered for duty in the Philippines. Chamberlin was part of the last naval group to escape from Corregidor. He was stationed in FRUMEL from May 1942 to October 1944. It is interesting to note that FRUMEL worked on Japanese diplomatic traffic, but Central Bureau did not handle this traffic. Chamberlin's description of life at FRUMEL and his work on the PURPLE machine presents an interesting picture of their activity there.

I learned cryptanalysis by taking a self-study course based on the writings of William Friedman. After I completed three sections of the course by myself, my supervisor made me a full-time student and I quickly completed the course. I volunteered for duty in the Philippines and worked in the diplomatic section on Corregidor. I learned the PURPLE machine in Washington, but a major part of my job on Corregidor was working on traffic from the RED machine. Commander Swede Carlson, an excellent teacher, taught me the RED machine. At this time, the Japanese used the PURPLE machine to encrypt communications from its embassies and the RED machine to encrypt communications from its consulates. As part of the last group to escape from Corregidor, I was very glad to get to Melbourne, Australia. I always felt a little guilty about making it to FRUMEL because some of my friends were stuck as prisoners of war in the Philippines.

When I arrived at FRUMEL in May 1942, there was no IBM equipment at the site yet. I got the second PURPLE machine that came from Washington. What a mess! The keys did not work as they should and the rotors went in all directions. I spent much time with a screwdriver and pliers, but I made the machine work perfectly by the time I was done.

Another frustrating part of my work was Washington's failure to send the daily keys on time. We always got them three or four days late. I got around this problem too. All I needed was two messages from Shanghai. I broke the plug setting down with the first message and confirmed it with the second message. We did not have enough cryptanalysts for round-the-clock shifts until more than a year after we came to Melbourne. One nice part about the start of round-the-clock work was that we finally got a full day off.

I enjoyed the work because we were always busy. We had so much intercept. Our material came from intercept sites at Adelaide River and Exmouth Gulf. The majority of our material came from the site at Moorabbin. Our work was very important. After the Pearl Harbor attack, the Navy communications branch was our first line of defense. Communications intelligence helped the U.S. determine when to pick a fight and when to avoid one. This information was especially crucial in 1942, when we were short on ships and men.

The officers who graduated from the Naval Academy worked either in the front office or in the translation section. The officers in the cryptanalysis section were naval reservists. Fabian, the commander, was a tough cookie. Once you understood him, however, he was not too bad.

When the Seventh Fleet moved MacArthur to the Philippines in October 1944, FRUMEL was too far away and [was] no longer needed for the war effort. I believe that FRUMEL was disbanded in the fall of 1944. When I returned to the States in 1944, I was stationed at Nebraska Avenue. I was amazed to see so many people working there. Fabian always told us we had to stay at FRUMEL and work hard because the Navy had no personnel to send here. I was treated well at Nebraska Avenue because of my overseas war service. I remained at Nebraska Avenue until I left the Navy in 1948. I came back to Nebraska Avenue as a civilian in 1949. I held several jobs at NSA such as cryptologic planning officer. I retired in 1969.

My experience at FRUMEL was especially rewarding because we worked closely with the translators on specific problems. We could see that our work was valued and appreciated. If we had been a larger unit, the work would have been more production-oriented.

I Was a Recovery Man

Robert Cahill enlisted in the naval reserves and was called to active duty in February 1942. Although he was at FRUMEL for a short time, he represents the experiences of the average cryptanalyst. It is remarkable that cryptanalysts such as Cahill were able to stick to difficult, boring tasks without feedback on what their work really accomplished. When Cahill left the Navy, he joined the National Security Agency as a cryptanalyst and retired in 1981.

I worked in the complaints department of the Commercial Freight Company in Columbus, Ohio. In our company, anyone who was about to be drafted went to see Charlie and he got you into the Navy. Charlie was Commander Ford's brother-in-law so it was easy to get work at OP-20-G, the Navy's cryptologic organization. I joined in February 1942 as a yeoman third class. I had no basic training. When I arrived in Washington, Commander Ford told me to go find a room and report to Ensign John Watson the next morning at 0700 hours. There were so many navy men coming to Washington that we got our uniforms in installments. I did not get a full uniform until June. I reported to the Navy building on Constitution Avenue.

On my first day of work, they gave me a pencil, and I started recovering additives. I was a recovery man for the rest of the war. The first system that I worked on was JN-25, a five-digit code system. First I looked for high-frequency code groups. Next, I made up an imaginary key that gave me the code groups to look for and then dragged it through pages and pages of traffic to see if I was correct. After the key was recovered, it was entered into the recovery book, which was a duplicate of the key book. Cryptanalysts either did key recovery or additive recovery. In key recovery, we align the messages so that we can get the starting point for decoding.

I suppose that I was placed in additive recovery work because my bachelor's degree was in business administration, which theoretically gave me a background in accounting. After a while, when I was still in Washington but at Nebraska Avenue, we got adding machines that looked like cash registers to help us do our work. These machines were good if there was no depth because they helped us try different possibilities. I found these machines to be too slow if there was depth because I could add faster by hand. After the additive was recovered, the information went to the translation section and was applied to the text. We knew that we made it possible to read messages, but that is all we knew. Translators sometimes asked us to check things because there was a hole in a message or a certain position looked invalid. I never saw a fully decrypted message. I never heard the word ULTRA. I knew nothing about the distribution of product. The only thing I knew was that we worked in communications intelligence. When I went overseas to

Melbourne and later to Hawaii, we had more contact with traffic analysts and translators, but secrecy was still strictly enforced.

I kept volunteering to go to Australia because I heard that it was a good place to work. Finally I was selected to go in July 1944. There was no mass influx of recruits to Melbourne. When a man was eligible to transfer because he had accumulated enough points, he was replaced. Since many of the men at FRUMEL were evacuated from Corregidor, their time was up in 1944. Not many ships were bound for Australia, so it took some time for me to get there. I went over on a refrigerator ship that contained the Thanksgiving dinners for all of the military in the Southwest Pacific theater.

I had a typical military bureaucratic situation surrounding my trip to Australia. Even though we were going to Australia, the Navy issued us full jungle gear because we had a Southwest Pacific address. Three yeomen [and I] were going to FRUMEL. The Navy gave each of us a pith helmet, jungle boots, and a complete green outfit that weighed over eighty pounds. When it was time to unload the ship at Manus Island so that we could transfer to the next ship, the chief called us and asked us how we were going to unload our crates. What crates? Each of us had a 125-pound crate that contained a pup tent, shovels, rifles, ammunition, and everything else that we needed to live in the jungle. They had to get a special truck each time we loaded and unloaded a ship. When we reached Brisbane and it was time to take the

train to Melbourne, we forgot those crates.

At FRUMEL, I continued to recover additives. Since I had replaced Chief Foster, who worked on the JN-11 system, I took over this system too. The JN-11 system was a four-digit code system that turned out to be very minor. We worked side by side with the Australians, which was most enjoyable. Our specialty was recovering messages about Japanese submarine movement. I knew very little Japanese, but I remember the charts of keywords that were available to help the analysts. I stayed at FRUMEL for only three months and left in December 1944 when the U.S. turned FRUMEL completely over to the Australians.

My next tour of duty was Pearl Harbor. After a few days of leave at home in the States, I left San Francisco for Hawaii. What a trip! I was on a Kaiser aircraft carrier with two decks packed full of planes to be transported for the Iwo Jima invasion. The ship was so full that it was extremely top-heavy. We had a terrible storm; the waves had to have been over fifty feet high because they came over the flight deck. There were so many sick crewmen that the passengers had to do guard duty. I did guard duty on the flight deck two nights during the storm. I was supposed to guard the planes. If a plane broke loose, I was to keep it from going overboard. Since flight decks have no rails, one false step and I would have been overboard. It was impossible to march around the deck, so we just sat in one of the planes in the middle of the group. Those two nights were two of the longest that I have ever experienced.

At Pearl [Harbor], I was once again in the recovery section. The Navy ran FRUMEL and FRUPAC in the same manner, so I had no trouble getting into the routine. Security was a little looser in FRUPAC because we worked in one big area and the traffic analysts were in the back of the room. In both Melbourne and Washington, we worked in smaller rooms behind closed doors so the sections were more isolated from each other. Even in FRUPAC, I never saw a fully decrypted message because of strict security. I did get to work on a special project at FRUPAC; I matched a Japanese key book that was picked up by the U.S. with material that we already recovered. It was gratifying to see how well we did and how few errors we had made.

We were busy right up to V-J Day. Although the pace of the war had slackened, the Japanese navy kept up its flow of messages. I will never forget the sight of Pearl Harbor when we thought the Japanese had surrendered. Every ship lit its flares. There was an aircraft carrier that had no flares, so they shot bullets in the air. We worked on the highest point overlooking Pearl Harbor [possibly Aliamanu Crater]. When the real surrender came a few days later, the harbor was quiet. We had no more flares to light or ammunition to shoot. It was great that the war was really over.

Keeping the Equipment Humming at FRUMEL

The Challenges of Running the IBM Operation at FRUMEL

Rear Admiral Ralph E. Cook received a bachelor's degree in electrical engineering from Montana State College in 1938. Throughout high school and college, Cook was an amateur radio operator and a member of the naval communications reserve. In January 1941, Cook was commissioned as an officer in the naval reserves. He worked for IBM as a field engineer until April 1941, when he was called to duty in the Navy. Admiral Cook's naval career spanned thirty-four years. After World War II, he remained in the SIGINT business and made important contributions in the research and development field. Cook held such positions as director of the Naval Security Group and commander of NSA/CSS Pacific.

Ralph Cook is one of the few Americans who served at FRUMEL for almost the entire war. He came to FRUMEL in May 1942 and did not leave until after V-J Day. He remained there even though the Americans officially turned FRUMEL over to the Australian navy in January 1945. Therefore, Cook provides a very complete picture of the operation. As the head of the IBM operation, Cook not only presents information on its challenges but also

Ralph E. Cook

demonstrates the complexities involved in cryptanalytic tasks. It is interesting to note that personnel at IBM operations at both Central Bureau and FRUMEL had a close relationship with the cryptanalysts. While neither organization coordinated with the other, both made similar advances in the use of IBM equipment to automate parts of the cryptanalytic process. See chapter 3, "The Key to Our Success Was Teamwork," by Charles Girhard.

I started out in the Navy standing watches, but found myself fixing enciphering equipment from time to time. I went to the Philippines in August 1941. When the intelligence personnel learned of my IBM background, I became the object of a fight between them and the district communications officer. After we moved from Cavite [the Philippines] to Corregidor in December 1941, they reached a compromise on my services. I worked eight hours for intelligence, eight hours for the general communications services, and the other eight hours for myself.

Lieutenant John Lietwiler, who was in charge of the intelligence unit, told me to mechanize as much of the cryptanalytic process as possible and to keep the equipment running. The IBM installation was already in operation on Corregidor, but they were glad to have my services for programming enhancements and equipment maintenance. They gave me ten days to learn the cryptanalytic process so that I could see what problems the analysts faced. I learned how to strip additives and to recover the key. I was introduced to the Japanese language so that I could recognize twenty commonly used words or code groups, such as addresses or opening phrases. Searching for a keyword or

code group helped us determine if the additive placement was correct. Fortunately, we had a good recovery list at this time. The basic code contained 10,000 code groups. However, you could read 80 percent of the traffic with 2,000 code groups. Since most of our traffic dealt with ship movements, there were frequently used phrases that helped us out. I created reference files of code and additive that the analysts found very helpful. My training and activities on Corregidor were a good preparation for the tasks that I faced at FRUMEL. I was part of the last group evacuated from Corregidor, and it was sure a relief to make it to Melbourne.

My first challenge at FRUMEL was to obtain IBM equipment. Although we packed our IBM equipment for shipment from Corregidor, we had to abandon it because there was not enough time to load it onto our evacuation submarine. The remaining troops were to dump it in the ocean if they could. I was glad that I had mixed parts from various machines in the same case. This made assembly difficult if the box ever got into the wrong hands. After a few months, the IBM equipment arrived from Washington, but the printing mechanism for the tabulator and the card feeder were missing. I could not order parts from the Australians because they had nothing; they did everything by hand. There was a British tabulating machine company in Melbourne. They were no help because their equipment was not compatible with ours. We punched up cards for three months, waiting for the missing parts to come from Washington.

My next challenge was to provide greater assistance to the analysts by automating more of the process. I wanted to do more than generate code groups and additives. The cryptanalysts still had to work the code into traffic form and then give it to the translators. Commander Fabian was scheduled to visit Washington. I asked him to try to get us a naval communications 4 [NC4] machine, a machine that could calculate false [noncarrying] addition. IBM created this machine specifically for the Navy. While waiting for Fabian's return, I continued to look for a solution to this problem. I got Commander Holtwick, Fabian's temporary replacement, to grant permission for me to experiment with the machines that we had. I took a big risk because I could have ruined the machines. I figured out how to make the tabulator do false [noncarrying] addition. I modified the equipment to process the traffic by applying the additive to the code group. Then the machine would place the Kana meaning [probably Romaji] next to the particular code group. Thus, we eliminated a manual step in making the traffic ready for translation. Now cryptanalysts could devote all of their time to developing the additive and recovering the key.

When Fabian returned from Washington, I asked him what the chances were of our getting an NC4 machine. He said none. There was only one machine and Washington was not about to send it out here. Fabian also stated that Washington said my idea of mechanizing the working of the code group through the traffic would not work. I said that

I was sorry to hear that. I subsequently informed Washington of these techniques.

The machine room was located in the garages at the Monterey Apartments. Obtaining enough work space was a terrible problem for everyone when we were located at these apartments. In 1944, the FRUMEL offices were moved to a building specifically built for us at Albert Park. When we moved to Albert Park, the size of the machine room was doubled. I also was able to get some additional equipment. Now we had ten keypunchers and three tabulators. Approximately fifty RAAN personnel and fifteen Americans kept the IBM operation going twenty-four hours a day. I believe that the IBM operation at FRUMEL was successful because I made sure that every machine operator knew the total cryptanalytic process. This understanding helped the operator recognize errors instead of compounding them by just going through the motions. The IBM operation in Washington was much different. Because of compartmentalization, each step was confined to a separate bay. The operator only knew his specific task. Therefore, errors could not be determined until the end of the process. This assembly line procedure caused much wasted work effort.

There was no coordination on machine processing between FRUMEL and Central Bureau. We even tried to keep the rest of the Navy ignorant of FRUMEL activities. One time, an inspector general from the Seventh Fleet wanted to visit us. The guard said, 'I cannot let you in, I'll call the commanding officer'. The inspector general left, but he was furious. He complained to the chief of staff for the Seventh Fleet, who told him to forget it and leave us alone.

FRUMEL made significant contributions to the war effort. One of our early successes was the discovery of the Japanese plan to attack Midway. FRUPAC takes credit for this feat, but FRUMEL found the first tip-off about this plan. I know what happened because I was an eyewitness.

One night, I was called in at 2200 hours to fix a machine. When I finished, I went to the cryptanalysis area to get a cup of coffee and to look for an empty desk where I might sleep. I could not go home because the street cars had already stopped running for the night.

It was customary for cryptanalysts to go through the traffic and pull up all of the solid or clean messages and toss the garbled messages in an empty cardboard IBM box. It was easier to strip the additive from clean messages. If time permitted, the analyst would work on the garbled traffic after completing the solid messages. P.O. William Trembly was an enlisted man who stripped additive. He started work on a half-filled box of garbled traffic by pulling out one sheet. As he stripped the additive, his interest was peaked when he noticed the word 'attack'. The placename Midway was also identified in the message that Trembly discovered. Trembly was lucky to happen on the most important piece of paper in the box. He was also smart enough to recognize what he had. Trembly brought the message to the watch officer and they began to look for other parts of the message. At

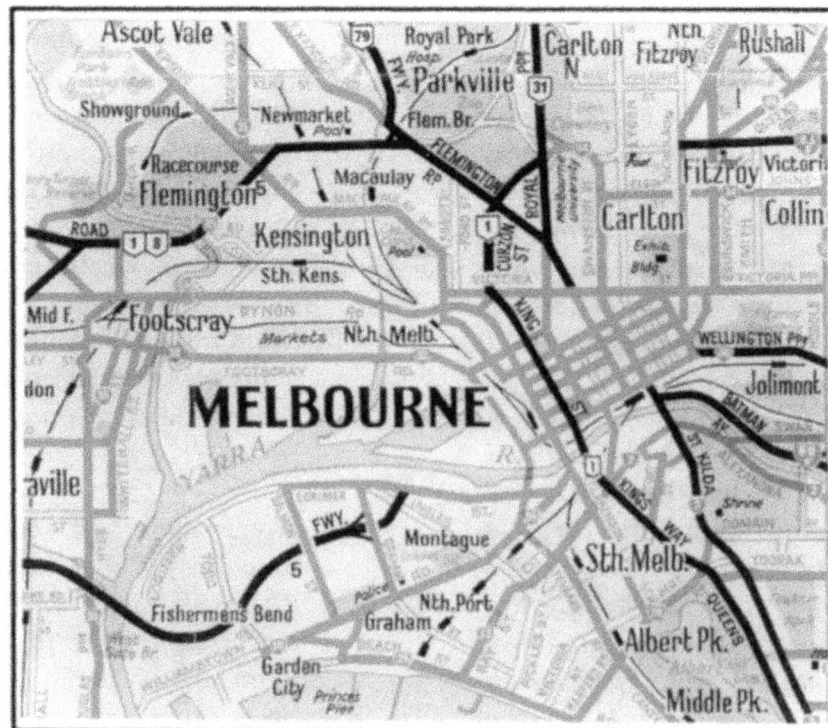

In 1944 FRUMEL moved to new expanded quarters at Albert Park.

FRUMEL, finished product was put out by the translators. Lieutenant Commander Gil Richardson sent this Midway attack plan to both Washington and FRUPAC. No station had a solid message. FRUPAC and Washington were able to solve parts of the message that we did not have, but the tip-off came from FRUMEL.

FRUMEL also made valuable contributions in support of the submarine missions out of Fremantle, Australia. These contributions continued as the war progressed and the Seventh Fleet headquarters moved north. Thanks to our information, submarines knew when and where to prey on Japanese ships. I have little first-hand knowledge of finished product because I was not involved in that part of the operation. Language officers, primarily Lieutenant Rufus Taylor and Lieutenant Commander Gil Richardson put out the final product. Lieutenant Commander Swede Carlson was another outstanding language officer at FRUMEL. It was unusual for Lieutenant Lietwiler, head of the intelligence section, to have two lieutenant commanders under him, but it was not a problem. Richardson and Carlson were extremely busy with their translation tasks. They were happy to leave the administrative duties to Lietwiler.

As is typical of the military, I had a half dozen other duties in addition to running the machine operations. One of these duties was marriage investigator. If an American wanted to marry an Australian, we conducted an investigation. We tried to keep everyone honest. We tried to protect the bride from a military man who pretended to have great wealth. Likewise we tried to protect the groom from a girl who just wanted a ticket to the U.S. In 1944 I got married to an Australian girl. I was obliged to wait six months, and another officer did my investigation.

I believe that we remained in Melbourne throughout the war because Melbourne was the headquarters of the Australian navy. The Australians did not want to move north. Toward the end of the war, the Americans turned all of our resources over to the Australians. I was one of a handful of Americans who stayed at FRUMEL until shortly after the Japanese surrender. Commander Jack Newman, the head of FRUMEL and the head of the RAAN unit, asked Washington if I could stay for an additional six months after the war. Washington had other plans. I came back to Nebraska Avenue to run its machine operation. Numerous challenges awaited me at the Naval Security Group.

Staying in Tune and Other Duties

Like Rear Admiral Cook, Lieutenant Commander Joseph L. McConnel arrived in Melbourne as part of the last group that was evacuated from Corregidor. McConnel was also at FRUMEL through V-J Day in August 1945. McConnel was responsible for a crucial part of the operation. He made sure that the receivers worked properly so that information could be intercepted and that the typewriters worked so that the information could be distributed. Here is his story.

In 1929, I joined the Navy and became a radio operator. After a few years at sea, I was selected for special training in Washington, D.C., in 1932. Before

Joseph L. McConnel

acceptance, I had an interview in West Virginia and had to demonstrate that I could copy code. I was glad that I did not have to send code because I never learned how to do it. I was a member of the eighth OTRG class and learned how to intercept Japanese naval communications. My first assignment was in Guam. Although I did intercept work, I fell into fixing equipment. As a child, I always enjoyed putting radio sets together. I did not have any training on fixing receivers. I just learned as I went along. After Guam, I stayed in the repair business or, as the Navy would say, material duty full-time.

During my time with FRUMEL, I was stationed at the intercept site at Moorabbin. I was responsible for a large variety of tasks. Since having power was a must, I maintained the emergency generator, a German product that ran on diesel fuel. Thank goodness it worked well. There were three types of receivers at Moorabbin: American HRO receivers,

Australian HRO receivers, and [Hallicrafters]. Obtaining parts was always a challenge. Frequently, I bought small parts locally from the open market because it was the quickest and easiest way to get them.

I had frustrating moments fixing receivers. For instance, one of the [Hallicrafters] receivers just would not stay tuned. It kept jumping frequencies. After much trial and error, I finally discovered a small microcondenser with varying capacity that was parallel with the oscillator section of the main tuning condenser. I disconnected the microcondenser and luckily the receiver settled down. Then I replaced the microcondenser.

Fixing the typewriters at Moorabbin was a one-man operation. The slugs on the typing bars were constantly falling off. I kept slugs in an open peanut can on my workbench until I had a chance to put them back on the typewriter. Those who smoked flicked their ashes in any available open container. As a result, during cleanup times, my slugs ended up in the trash. I went through the trash and found every one of those little slugs. Since they were made of hard metal, they did not disintegrate when the trash was burned. From then on, I never left an open container on my workbench.

I also helped with the photographing of captured Japanese code books. At first, we developed the pictures ourselves as we had on Corregidor. The workload became overwhelming so we sought outside help. At first, we took the films to an Australian commercial cinema for processing.

Naturally, for security reasons, we stayed in the cinema and never let those films out of our sight. Eventually, we took the film to an Australian army photography lab.

I enjoyed working with RAAN personnel and learned a good lesson from them. They were not used to buildings with central heating as the Americans were. For the first year, we argued about whether the windows should stay open or closed. Since there were more Americans, we won and the windows stayed closed. I noticed that we had colds and the RAAN personnel did not. During the second year, the windows stayed closed and we all had colds. To this day, I keep my home on the cool side.

Life was good to me during the FRUMEL years. I received two promotions to warrant officer and then to ensign. I also found my wife. Our marriage was a tricky affair. I was transferred back to the states, to the intercept site at Bainbridge, Washington, late in 1944. If I did not get back to Australia to marry my fiancee, she would have had a difficult time coming to the U.S. Fortunately, the Navy sent me back to Melbourne in 1945. I got married and stayed in Moorabbin until the end of the war. I was transferred to Hawaii and my wife was able to join me there.

After a variety of assignments as material officer and in research and development, I left the Navy in 1959.

Life at Frumel from a Linguist's Perspective

Rear Admiral Gil McDonald Richardson graduated from the Naval Academy in 1927. After several years at sea, Richardson was selected to study Japanese in the Navy's three-year Tokyo program. Richardson's description of his Japanese training is very interesting. The contrast between the Navy and Army training programs is quite remarkable. See chapter 4, "A Central Bureau J-Boy" and "A Bizarre Experiment." The Navy had a strong Japanese language training program to prepare for war in the 1930s. The Army played catch-up and had to train its linguists while the war was in progress. Richardson also attests to the dedication to duty of all of the participants at FRUMEL. He and other linguists served under a junior officer so that they could devote all of their time and energy to Japanese translation rather than to administrative duties.

Gil McDonald Richardson

I always liked to study languages. In my high school days and when I attended the Naval Academy, I studied Spanish. However, I applied for the Navy's Japanese training pro-

gram to distinguish myself from the pack and to improve my promotion chances. I arrived in Tokyo to begin my three years of study in November 1935.

The Navy set up a rigorous program of study for us. We had five tutors who worked with us every day. We read everything from children's books to the Japanese daily press. The tutors took us on field trips to expose us to a variety of situations in which to practice the language. We had an exam every six months to demonstrate our progress. Passing the exam was not enough. If you did not get a thirty-four, the Navy sent you home with an unsatisfactory fitness report. By the end of the course, we were required to read 2,800 Kanji [Chinese characters that have been incorporated into the Japanese language] characters and to write 1,800 Kanji characters.

The only criticism that I had of the program was that the instructors wanted us to learn by listening and memorizing the language. They could not give us grammar rules or explanations because their knowledge of English was limited. I bought myself a Japanese grammar book that was written in English, which was invaluable to me. By the end of the program, we were qualified translators and interpreters.

We did not have much direct supervision from the Navy. We were under the naval attaché at the embassy. I especially remember Captain Bemus, one of the naval attachés, because he invited us to do espionage from time to time. I was young and had no

fear so I volunteered as much as possible. I had a variety of espionage activities. For example, I went to northern Japan to determine how many tunnels were constructed along a railway. Another time, I went to Nagasaki to determine if the Japanese were building battleships in violation of the London Treaty. I found that the Japanese were building a battleship with eighteen-inch gun turrets and [that] they were building a light aircraft carrier.

I got into some interesting predicaments on these espionage trips. On my way home from Nagasaki, I found that I had no money for my train ticket. I asked the conductor to phone my cook to meet me at the station. The Japanese cook lent me the money. I wanted to reward him for showing up at the station so I offered to treat him to lunch at a classy Japanese restaurant.

When we got there, I realized I was expected to take off my shoes. I could not do this because my shoes were full of secret documents! I quickly suggested that I treat him to a foreign restaurant because he could have Japanese food at any time. He bought this excuse and the day was saved.

I had a special passport to use for these special assignments, which stated that I was a friend of the prime minister. Frequently, policemen who stopped to question me about why I was in a certain location could not read this passport because it was written in court or fancy Japanese. I had to read it to them and eventually the police were satisfied, but I had some close calls.

Toward the end of our studies, we went to Korea to serve as interpreters for embassy personnel who carried secret mail back and forth to our consulates. Japan occupied Korea during this period. I enjoyed the espionage and other special assignments because they not only provided opportunities for me to use Japanese, but also provided a valuable service for the U.S. by acquiring information.

I completed my studies and left Japan in November 1938. After working on Japanese codes at Pearl Harbor, I went to Manila as Admiral Hart's intelligence officer. Toward the end of 1940, Redfield Mason asked me to go to Corregidor because traffic was on the rise and they only had one translator. I was delighted to go and became very involved with this challenging work.

I was part of the second group that was evacuated from Corregidor in March 1942. I credit Admiral Hart, head of the Asiatic Fleet, for making it possible for us to escape from Corregidor. Admiral Hart ordered all submarines with a mission in the area to replenish their fuel and torpedoes at Corregidor. Earlier, an oil tanker, which had run aground at Monkey Point, became the source of fuel for the submarines. Before the war began, all of the torpedoes were removed from Cavite and stored in the tunnel on Corregidor. Thus, torpedoes were available for the submarines. The last task that each sub carried out at Corregidor was to take military personnel from Corregidor to a safer haven.

I was a part of FRUMEL in Melbourne, Australia, from the spring of 1942 until the end of 1944. I enjoyed working with the Australians very much and we worked well together, 'like a hand in a glove'. There were no Australian linguists at FRUMEL, but we were ably assisted by Lieutenant Commander Meriman from the British navy, who had escaped from Singapore. We followed the same working procedures that we had on Corregidor. Swede Carlson, a Japanese linguist who graduated from the Navy Tokyo program in 1936, and I were lieutenant commanders at this time and were senior to Rudy Fabian. We continued our arrangement with Fabian that was worked out on Corregidor. Fabian was to be the boss or commander in charge even though he was junior to us. This arrangement freed Carlson and me from administrative duties and allowed us to devote all of our time and energy to translation and code recovery. Everyone, especially me, was satisfied with this arrangement.

I found the work at FRUMEL fascinating. Translating and assisting with code recovery is like reading a great book that you just cannot put down. I remember working late into the night on messages relating to the Japanese plan to attack Midway. I also remember working on Yamamoto's schedule, which led to the shootdown of his plane. The message that I worked on was in a Japanese army code system. Although we were unfamiliar with Japanese army codes, we got this message out in a hurry because it was a substitution system.

When I left Melbourne in 1944, I returned to Washington and continued translation and code recovery work until September 1945. I left the Navy in 1957. My work on the Japanese naval problem was one of the major highlights of my career.

MELBOURNE

Melbourne (untitled photo)

Melbourne's "Dog on the Tucker Box." The inscription: "Earth's self upholds this monument to conquerers who won her when winning was dangerous, and now are gathered unto her again."

Part of the beauty of Melbourne lay in its botanical gardens.

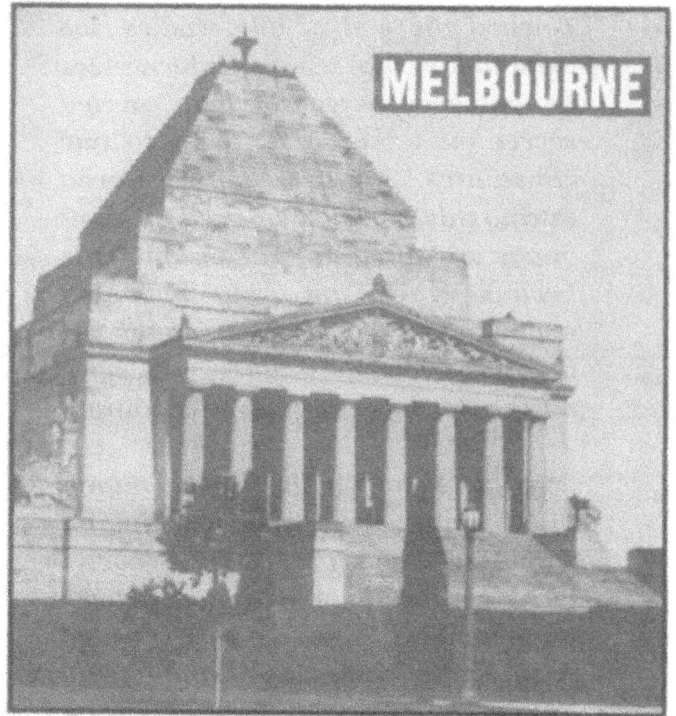

This statue is Melbourne's tribute to the Marquis of Linlithgow, first governor general of Australia.

Chapter 7
FRUMEL and Central Bureau: A Comparison

The Southwest Pacific theater obtained information from two communications intelligence organizations, Central Bureau and FRUMEL, which were actually located in the theater. A comparison of these organizations not only sheds light on their operations, but also strengthens our understanding of the significant role that communications intelligence played in the war effort.

The selections in this chapter show that Central Bureau and FRUMEL had similar missions of gathering intelligence from Japanese communications. While Central Bureau gathered intelligence from Japanese army-ground and both army and naval air communications, FRUMEL gathered intelligence only from Japanese naval communications. In the winter of 1943, the Navy turned the army water transport problem over to the Army for solution. The breaking of this code is one of the highlights of Central Bureau's success. (See chapter 3 of this history.)

While both organizations were joint military organizations with the Australians, FRUMEL was very small in comparison to Central Bureau. FRUMEL had a few hundred personnel, while Central Bureau had 4,339 personnel by the end of the war. FRUMEL not only had fewer logistical problems because of its size, but also remained in Melbourne and did not move forward with general headquarters as Central Bureau did. As an army organization, Central Bureau had more resources since Major General Spencer B. Akin was director of both Central Bureau and MacArthur's signal corps. The directors of FRUMEL were only lieutenants and had more difficulties obtaining resources from the Navy. (See chapter 6, "A Conversation with the Operators.") Consequently, while both organizations had field sections or forward units, Central Bureau's coverage was more extensive.

The following excerpts illustrate the complex relationships between each service. Because of the technical difficulties that each organization faced, it worked cooperatively with its own cryptologic organization in Washington, D.C.: Central Bureau with Arlington Hall and FRUMEL with OP-20-G. There is more evidence of turf battles within the Navy over the organizational placement of communications intelligence. There was much less cooperation on an interservice level.

Although both organizations performed intercept, traffic analysis, cryptanalysis and translation tasks, there were significant differences in their day-to-day operations. The following interviews demonstrate that some disagreements came about because of the general differences between the methods of doing business in the U.S. Army and the U.S. Navy. For example, FRUMEL was more directly involved in distribution of its product than was Central Bureau. Central Bureau gave everything to General Akin, who determined its distribution. Other differences occurred because of individual personalities and leadership styles, yet both organizations were very successful. FRUMEL was able to provide information to the Allies throughout the war because the Navy had studied Japanese naval codes prior to the war and had the necessary background and continuity. Another advantage for FRUMEL was that the Americans who came there were a cohesive unit that worked together on Japanese naval codes at station Cast on Corregidor. The Cast organization merely joined the Australian SIGINT organization. In contrast, the U.S. Army began its study of Japanese army codes only when the war began because prior to the war it had concentrated its codebreaking efforts on the Japanese diplomatic code. Consequently, Central Bureau did not read mainline Japanese army codes until March 1944. While FRUMEL was formed from an existing organization of Americans, Central Bureau was formed in part by creating a new organization within the U.S. Army.

The recollections of Colonel Sinkov, Captain Rudolph Fabian, and Captain E. S. L. Goodwin give interesting overviews of their respective organizations. Their leadership styles were very different, but all were effective. Fabian and Goodwin, career military officers who joined the Navy in 1928 and 1921, respectively, ran FRUMEL in rigid military fashion. Sinkov, on the other hand, was more of a professor than a commander despite his military experience in the reserves dating back to 1932. All came to their tasks with much experience in cryptanalysis. Sinkov was hired as a civilian by the Signals Intelligence Service in 1930, and he learned cryptanalysis from the master, William Friedman. Sinkov was at Central Bureau from July 1942 until the end of the war. Fabian was selected by Commander Safford and joined OP-20-G in the late 1930s. After studying cryptanalysis, he went to the Philippines in 1940 to command the intercept unit at Corregidor. Fabian was at FRUMEL from the spring of 1942 until September 1943. Goodwin began his cryptologic career in Washington in 1932 and had cryptologic assignments in Washington and the Philippines. His cryptologic career was periodically interrupted by tours of sea duty. Goodwin relieved Fabian and left FRUMEL in September 1944. Examining the recollections of these men is instructive because they provide interesting comparisons of both organizations.

Security Was a Paramount Concern

Rudolph T. Fabian graduated from the Naval Academy in 1931. After several years of sea duty, he was selected for cryptographic school in Washington, D.C., in 1938. As commander of the naval unit at Corregidor from 1940 to 1942, Fabian was involved in the intense search for information on the Japanese plans prior to the Pearl Harbor attack. He also had to cope with the difficulties created by the rapid Japanese advance through the Philippines in late 1941 and early 1942. Since Fabian was at FRUMEL from its beginnings in 1942 until 1943, he is a good source of information on its operations and accomplishments.

I received a letter from Commander Laurance Safford inviting me to Washington to work with his organization. I accepted the offer even though I did not know what he had in mind because I did not get accepted for graduate work in ordnance as I had hoped. Commander Safford had my name taken off the ordnance school list so that I could work in his program. Commander Safford was a brilliant man. Many people disliked him because he was so quick. I was in a class of three people so our instruction was very intense. It was most fortuitous that Redfield (Rosie) Mason, a Japanese linguist, taught us Japanese telegraph codes as part of our class. After studying cryptanalysis, I spent a short time at

Rudolph T. Fabian

Constitution Avenue because the Navy made it a practice to rotate officers out to the field after a year. With the start of war, my stint in the field turned out to be a long one.

I escaped from Corregidor and went to Melbourne in February 1942. We set up headquarters at the Monterey Apartments. FRUMEL was officially established on 12 March 1942. My counterpart from the RAN [Royal Australian Navy] was Captain Jack Newman. The Australians were very helpful; their analysts and linguists were very talented.

Our mission was navy communications. We did everything from beginning to end – decryption, translation, and processing. The JN-25 systems that we worked on were very complex. The first thing we had to do was find the start of the message. Sometimes the beginning of the message would be in the middle of the paragraph or sometimes it would be at the end of the message. We had to find the starting point and then double back. One clue that helped us was that code values were divisible by three.

To enhance our ability to solve the Japanese naval systems, we shared information with our sister naval cryptologic units. We had a secure communications system called the COPAC system, which enabled us to share information with the Fleet Radio Unit Pacific [FRUPAC], Washington, London, and the British Eastern Fleet. These sites worked well together. As the commander of FRUMEL, I kept our material circulating in the COPAC all the time.

Security was a paramount concern for me. I was relieved when Commander Nave, an Australian cryptanalyst, left FRUMEL for Central Bureau. He left because I reprimanded him for his lack of security. I also had to get my admiral to remind MacArthur about the need for security. MacArthur was so exuberant about our warning him that the Japanese were really going to attack Port Moresby, New Guinea, in 1942, that I feared he was going to reveal the source. I thought the U.S. Navy made a serious mistake when they shot down Admiral Yamamoto's plane in the spring of 1943. I believe that the risks to our security were too great. The Japanese could have discovered our intercept capabilities, and the outcome of the war may have been very different. FRUMEL played no role in this event because we were not in range to intercept Admiral Yamamoto's plans.

FRUMEL was assigned to the Asiatic Fleet and we worked for them. We distributed our information directly to Submarine Pacific Command and to the Fremantle unit. We also brought information once a day to the fleet intelligence officer at Brisbane. As MacArthur was the theater commander, we also supplied information directly to him. We strictly observed the need-to-know principle, but any commander who needed our information received it.

I want to respond to two questions. First, how did FRUMEL and Central Bureau get along? We just went our separate ways. We were not discouraged from communicating with the Army, but there was no agreement to *do so. FRUMEL did not handle any army air corps COMINT work. With regard to the question of why FRUMEL did not move up to Brisbane with MacArthur, I think they felt there was no advantage for us to move. We were in a good position for intercepting communications. We also had a good setup for space at Melbourne.*

FRUMEL made major valuable contributions during the Coral Sea battle, the Midway battle, and the fighting at Port Moresby, New Guinea. We also contributed piecemeal information to all of the naval battles in the Pacific. It was difficult for us to function because the Atlantic war took precedence over us in terms of supplies and manpower. Nevertheless, we did our job extremely well and made valuable contributions to the war effort.

In 1943, I was sent to Colombo, Ceylon [now Sri Lanka], as a liaison officer to provide COMINT to the British. I came back to the U.S. in 1945 and served as a staff officer at Nebraska Avenue at OP-20-G. After the war, I went back to sea on a cruiser. I had to leave intelligence work and go to sea in order to get further promotions. I left the Navy in 1961. My service in the COMINT world was a very rewarding part of my military career.

Communications Intelligence Has Many Dimensions

Captain Goodwin graduated from the Naval Academy in 1925. He went to sea for seven years and began his cryptologic career in 1932. After studying cryptanalysis for one year, Sid Goodwin became the head of OP-20-GC, the branch that created U.S. naval codes. Next Goodwin worked at station Cast in the Philippines from 1934 to 1936. From 1938 to 1940, Goodwin worked under Commander Safford as the head of OP-20-GY, the cryptanalysis branch of OP-20-G. After the war, Goodwin represented the Navy on the USCICC (Communications Intelligence Coordinating Committee), which assisted with the formation of AFSA, and he later served as AFSA's adjutant general. Goodwin was also the first inspector general for NSA. He left the Navy in 1956.

Commander Safford, although eccentric, was a genius. Safford introduced cryptanalysis to the Navy and established its intercept sites. Safford's greatest contributions were developing the ECM machine [Navy's version of SIGABA] and ensuring that this machine was ready when the war started. He was also responsible for the excellent communications security that the Navy had throughout the war. There are many dimensions to communications intelligence; therefore, we should be careful in judging its effectiveness. In 1932, when I took the cryptanalysis course set up by

E. S. L. Goodwin

Safford, I felt it was short on theory. My instructor was Tommy Dyer. We learned by just doing problems. However, when I was head of the cryptanalysis section, from 1938 to 1940, I did nothing to correct this situation. In 1943, before going to Melbourne to relieve Rudy Fabian, I came to Washington to brush up on the business. I had been at sea in 1941 and 1942. I was very impressed with the advances in codebreaking that I saw in 1943.

As a joint military organization, FRUMEL always had a U.S. commander and an Australian commander. Commander Jack Newman was the Australian commander throughout the war. Newman's duties were to monitor FRUMEL output for the Australians, help FRUMEL obtain resources, assist FRUMEL with the maintenance of good relationships with other sectors of the Australian government, and administer the two units of RAANs under FRUMEL control. One unit of RAANs was stationed at Moorabbin and the other was at our headquarters in Melbourne. Melbourne was also the headquarters for the RAN, and Newman was responsible for all naval communications out of Melbourne. When Fabian was commander, there was a triumvirate of Fabian, Lietwiler, and Newman. Lietwiler was never commander of FRUMEL by himself. All of us had excellent relations with Jack Newman. Working with the Australians was a great experience. My replacement, Commander Willcott, who handled the withdrawal of U.S. troops and functions from FRUMEL, had a few rough spots, which is understandable.

Our mission at FRUMEL was to obtain and process intercept on Japanese naval communications from Moorabbin. During my watch, 90 percent of our traffic was Japanese submarine communications. We also identified targets for our ships, such as Japanese oil tankers and troop ships. We gave our intelligence to both U.S. and Australian navy commanders.

Sometimes, because of atmospheric conditions, we intercepted FRUPAC targets. Then we would radio this traffic to station Hypo in Hawaii. In Australia, as in all British Commonwealth countries, the postmaster general was in charge of telegraph communications. The Melbourne postmaster general gave us control of a dedicated line to communicate with Hawaii and with Washington.

Working at FRUMEL was challenging because of the push-pull relationship it had with the Office of Naval Intelligence and the Office of Naval Communications. McCullom, the intelligence officer for the Seventh Fleet, wanted FRUMEL under his jurisdiction. Redman and Wenger, who were in the Office of Naval Communications, strongly resisted McCullom's efforts. They maintained that FRUMEL belonged under the Office of Naval Communications because its mission was communication techniques, and it was manned by communicators who depended on contacts with other communications units and the assistance of Japanese language officers. FRUMEL was established by an agreement between U.S. Navy communicators and the

Australian [Commonwealth] Naval Board. A shift by the U.S. Navy to move FRUMEL under the Office of Naval Intelligence could disrupt this agreement.

How much did FRUMEL contribute to the cryptologic effort in the Pacific? Those who worked in Hawaii say that they did 80 percent of the work. Others say that Washington did 75 percent of the work. Quantifying communications intelligence in this manner is incorrect. Communications intelligence is multidimensional not unidimensional. For instance, there are many categories of substantive contributions. Categories range from technical information to operational information. Operational intelligence can be divided further into the categories of background or planning versus tactical information needed by the field immediately. It is equally inappropriate to ask which site was number one in reading messages. Merely reading messages is not relevant. The important questions are, What messages were read? How timely were messages read? Which recipients got the messages? I believe that the entire team of FRUMEL, Hawaii, and Washington performed an inestimable service for the war effort. My time and contacts at FRUMEL were extremely gratifying and rewarding.

An Overview from the Commander/Professor

Colonel Abraham Sinkov, who began his study of cryptanalysis in 1930, was the most experienced cryptanalyst to serve in Australia. He offered leadership and continuity to Central Bureau because he served there from the summer of 1942 until the end of the war. He was not only extremely skilled in

working with a diverse work force but was also able to maintain high morale despite the complexity of Central Bureau's mission.

By the time I arrived in Melbourne in early 1942, the Australian group was already established at Central Bureau. There were two Australian contingents, an army contingent headed by Colonel Sanford and an air force contingent headed by Wing Commander Booth. The Australian contingent that we found in Melbourne when we arrived was largely a group recalled from North Africa. They had experience in traffic analysis, and they continued to work in that general direction. My arrival resulted in the existence of three separate working groups. There was a small American contingent, about a half dozen men, who preceded me. Additional personnel kept coming from Washington in groups. By the time we moved to Brisbane in September 1942, we had a fair size American group.

The reason we came to Melbourne originally was that Brisbane was actually the first line of defense. There was concern that the Japanese might invade Australia. After the Australian forces thwarted the Japanese attempt to cross the Owen Stanley Ranges and come toward Moresby, New Guinea, thus eliminating the fears of invasion, MacArthur moved his headquarters to Brisbane. Consequently, Central Bureau moved up to Brisbane in September 1942.

Central Bureau was a signals intelligence organization with responsibility for both cryptanalysis and traffic analysis. We used whatever means we could to develop signals intelligence. I don't recall that we ever had any indication from General Akin on matters of priority. Our priority was to get whatever signals intelligence we could from all of the traffic that was available to us. There was much collaboration between the American and Australian contingents right from the start of Central Bureau. In the fall of 1943, I became the head of Central Bureau. Now I was responsible for the whole thing, not just the American contingent. My good relations with the Australians did not change with this promotion.

Central Bureau's personnel were very diverse. In addition to Americans and Australians, some British who escaped from Singapore, some New Zealanders, and later on, some Canadians all worked at Central Bureau. American women who served with the WACs, Australian women who served with the WAAAFs, and the AWAS also played a vital role in our organization. Although the group was very diverse, we worked very well together. Unfortunately, when Central Bureau moved to the Philippines from May to July 1945, we lost the services of the WAAAFs and the AWAS. Under Australian law, women were not permitted to serve outside their continent. General Akin and I appealed for a waiver to Australian officials in Canberra, but our request was denied. Day-to-day operations ran very smoothly. I established general procedures so everyone knew what was expected of them. My role was both teacher and supervisor. Because of my cryptanalytic experience, I remained very involved with the technical aspects of our work. There was no distinction between Americans or Australians. Assignments were based on talent. Rank was not important; perform-

APPENDIX A.

TOP SECRET
ULTRA

PERSONNEL STRENGTH.
As of 15th August, 1945.

	U.S. ARMY	AIR	CANADIAN ARMY	NAVY	OTHER SERVICES	TOTALS.
CENTRAL BUREAU						
OFFICERS	101	17	1	35	3	157
	2 (WACs)	7 (AWAS)		1 (WAAFs)		10
EM	490	168	4	528		990
EW	157	42		96		294
CIVILIANS		1				1
TOTALS	750	235	5	459	3	1452
OFFICERS	28	44	10	45		158
		1 (AWAS)				1
EM	867	455	514	1069		2755
EW	17					17
TOTALS	915	525	535	1114	3	2907
GRAND TOTALS	1665	760	555	1575	5	4559

New Zealand Army and

TOP SECRET
ULTRA

Central Bureau was a large, complex operation requiring a wide range of diverse personnel. (Appendix A, Central Bureau World War II Technical Reports.)

ance certainly was important. It was fortunate that SIS or SSA [in 1943, the Signals Intelligence Service became the Signals Security Agency] had permission from the War Department to select personnel from the top intelligence level so we were assured of capable American personnel. Australia also followed this practice.

Central Bureau supervised intercept activities in the sense that the missions of the individual intercept groups were properly managed to avoid duplication of effort. Colonel Brown, who served with MacArthur in the Philippines and escaped to Australia in April 1942, was head of the intercept control group within Central Bureau. The only cryptologic effort that was not under Central Bureau jurisdiction was a small program in Sydney, Australia, called Service of Supply. This unit provided the cryptographic material for communications within the services. The unit's activities were not cryptanalytic in character.

The question arises as to why there was a general division of labor between the Australians and the Americans. First, the Australians worked in traffic analysis all along. Additionally, the Australian groups did not have any cryptanalytic experience. Therefore, the Americans performed most of the cryptanalysis. Later on, American intercept companies joined the effort operating primarily in New Guinea and the Philippines. How was intelligence produced by Central Bureau disseminated? We gave everything that was the least bit important to General

Akin. He received a daily delivery of our decrypts.

I am not informed at all as to what happened from there on, or to what extent General Akin provided material to General Willoughby, the head of MacArthur's G-2 section, or to General Sutherland, MacArthur's chief of staff. Central Bureau's responsibility, as directed by General Akin, to whom we reported directly, was that the material was to come to him. He then acted on it. We did have intelligence analysts who synthesized and analyzed decrypted materials. These intelligence summaries contained appreciations of important topics, such as strength of forces at a particular location, conditions of supplies, and general statements of morale. These summaries were also brought to General Akin.

I understand that there is confusion as to Central Bureau's role in the dissemination of intelligence. Let me emphasize this point – Central Bureau was an isolated installation on the edge of the city and separate from MacArthur's headquarters. Central Bureau did not disseminate information to operational units, to commanders, or to General Willoughby. Dissemination was General Akin's responsibility. Throughout the entire war, I met General Willoughby on only one occasion. After our victory at Leyte, General Sutherland summoned us to a conference on procedures. My counterpart in the Navy, Captain Munson, General Willoughby, and a few other generals and I were present. I had to go from Brisbane to the Philippines, approximately 3,500 miles each way, for a half-hour conference. General Sutherland should have just written me a letter.

Another criticism of the cryptanalytic effort during the war was too much duplication. There was duplication, but I really don't know how much duplication. Washington had more material to work with than we did at Central Bureau. In addition to all of our intercepts that we sent to Washington, Washington had material from other sources. The provision of cryptanalytic or intelligence results was only one way, from Central Bureau to Washington. Washington gave me no indication of any duplication problem and, besides, the duplication question had no relevance [to] our performance. Central Bureau's mission was to produce the maximum amount of intelligence that it could from the available intercepted material.

What was our relationship with other signals intelligence organizations? There was a cryptanalytic effort in the CBI [China-Burma-India] theater, and I corresponded with them. In contrast, relations between Central Bureau and Fleet Radio Unit Melbourne were nonexistent. No material from Melbourne came to us at Central Bureau. Nothing from Central Bureau went to Melbourne, not even technical material or information copies of important decrypts. The two problems were completely separate. The Navy worked on altogether different traffic from the traffic that Central Bureau dealt with. I made no attempt to establish contact with FRUMEL. I had no instructions in that connection, but it just seemed

to work out that way. We were just in two entirely different worlds.

My last assignment in connection with World War II was the TICOM operation. TICOM was a joint U.S.-British project to study enemy capabilities in signals intelligence. After the war ended, Colonel Erskine, a competent linguist, and I received a special assignment. We had to track down Japanese personnel who were involved in their communications activity. We tried to obtain information about Japanese procedures for developing cryptographic systems, about any successes that they had against American material or any other information related to signals intelligence. We had great trouble tracking down any appropriate individuals. We made very little headway because we had strict instructions that we were not to disclose to the Japanese any information about American successes.

So, when the Japanese lied to us, we could not reveal that we knew they were lying. Our counterparts in Germany were much more successful because when Germany surrendered, American troops were on the scene immediately and the Germans had no time to destroy their cryptographic material. In contrast, Japan surrendered on 15 August 1945, but American troops did not enter Japan until September. The Japanese had ample time to destroy their cryptographic material.

General Akin invited me to stay on in Japan, but I was anxious to go home to my new wife. I returned to the U.S. and Arlington Hall in February 1946.

Chapter 8
Walking a Tightrope

In war, there are many tightropes that the military must walk. There is the obvious one of danger from the enemy and many other not so obvious tightropes. Many of these situations are created by rivalries and political considerations. Even in World War II, the military services were large bureaucracies. The services were subject to the same political rivalries that we see in today's large corporations and government agencies. Fighting for control of resources and building fiefdoms were as common in World War II as they are today.

The problems experienced by the formation of joint military organizations are similar to the problems brought about by company mergers. Both situations heighten turf battles, increase rivalries, and can create confusion among managers. Forming a joint military organization under the pressure of war is especially difficult. Good communication was essential at Central Bureau not only because it was a joint military organization consisting of the U.S. Army, the Australian Imperial Forces, and the Royal Australian Air Forces, but also because its director had other duties and was not located on the premises. In addition to being the director of Central Bureau, Major General Spencer B. Akin was also MacArthur's chief signals officer. Mistakes were bound to occur in any joint military organization such as Central Bureau. It is remarkable that things ran as smoothly as they did.

Intelligence organizations had an additional tightrope in World War II. Military commanders who were consumers did not understand the value of the information available through SIGINT. They had to be convinced of its usefulness and learn to properly evaluate it. SIGINT personnel in the Southwest Pacific theater had to teach and persuade their commanders of the value of their product. This was a formidable task because by nature most human beings fear the unknown and resist change. The task was further complicated if the information came from a different branch of the service, army ground versus army air forces. Developing trust was a slow process especially between services. Could the Army trust information it received from the Navy and vice versa? The relations between Central Bureau and FRUMEL are a good illustration of this problem.

The following excerpts illustrate all of these problems: the mistrust of SIGINT, intra- and interservice rivalries, and difficulties within a joint military organization such as Central Bureau. "Persuading the Consumers" illustrates the mistrust and misunderstanding surrounding SIGINT. Brown's comments in "Managing Traffic Analysis with Akin at the Helm" point out the difficulties in the early years of the war in developing a joint military organization. Brown's tightrope was created by a lack of communication between General Akin and Wing Commander H. Roy Booth. Ballard's comments in "I Was the Meat in the Sandwich" point out the difficulties in the later years caused by the ever-increasing pace of the war. Ballard had to decide whether to follow the orders of General Akin at the war front or to follow the orders of his superiors at Central Bureau Brisbane.

Persuading the Consumers of the Value of SIGINT

The following comments by Colonel Howard W. Brown, Captain Rudolph T. Fabian, and Captain Duane L. Whitlock illustrate the shaky ground on which SIGINT stood during the early years of World War II. Commanders had to be persuaded and educated about this invaluable resource. Accurate predictions were the best remedy for this suspicion. Whitlock discusses a further complication – sometimes the consumer accepts cryptana-lytic evidence but is reluctant to accept intelligence based on traffic analysis. These three men were stationed in the Philippines and were evacuated from Corregidor. Although all three served in Australia, Brown was part of Central Bureau, while Fabian and Whitlock were part of FRUMEL.. Brown also illustrates intraservice rivalry while Fabian points to interservice rivalry.

Brown comments on the dark days in the Philippines after the Pearl Harbor disaster. The Japanese began bombing the Philippines on 8 December 1941. Fabian and Whitlock comment on the battles of the Coral Sea and Midway, two pivotal battles of the war in the Pacific. The Coral Sea battle, which began on 5 May 1942, not only blocked the Japanese invasion of Port Moresby, New Guinea, but also prevented the Japanese from isolating Australia from its source of U.S. supplies. The battle of Midway, which began on 3 June 1942, was the turning point for the naval war in the Pacific. The loss of Midway, the gateway to Hawaii, deprived the Japanese of an important foothold.

Brown: After Pearl Harbor, the Japanese moved quickly against the Philippines. They began bombing Manila on 9 December. Nichols Airfield and numerous U.S. airplanes that were on the ground were destroyed. The U.S. naval base at Cavite fell on 10 December. This period was a time of great frustration for me. We did our jobs, but others let us down.

On the afternoon of 9 December, radio intelligence got its first good break. Lieutenant Gelb and I were searching for enemy nets. I picked up a net that was using a great deal of plain Kana. One station sent numbers to the other between three to ten minute intervals. The numbers decreased rapidly until they reached

the 180 point. We figured out that these numbers were bearings. One of these 'stations' was actually a plane moving in our direction. I called Major Scherr, informed him that the plane or planes were up for two hours and asked for instructions. He told me to notify the air warning people. I called air warning but received a chilly reception. Their response was, 'that is interesting' and then they hung up. Our warning was correct. The bombs were definitely dropped.

Within a short time we were able to construct the whole net. The net became active again at 1300 on 10 December. I called air warning and told them that 100 'heavies' were in the air headed in our direction. Their response was, 'that is very interesting'. Later that afternoon, I called air warning again and told them to start blowing their whistles because the Japanese would be around in fifteen minutes. They said they were sorry, but since none of their observers spotted any planes, they hesitated to sound the alert. A few minutes later, our naval base at Cavite was not worth more than that much of unimproved land.

On the morning of the 15th or 16th of December, I called air warning and told them that the Japanese were on the way with an estimated arrival time of 1120. I also told them that the Japanese were pulling a new trick by coming down the eastern side of Luzon. According to our calculations, the planes would come in at twenty to twenty-five degrees. The planes came but without benefit of an alert. Later, when I called air warning to ask why they did not believe me, they said that

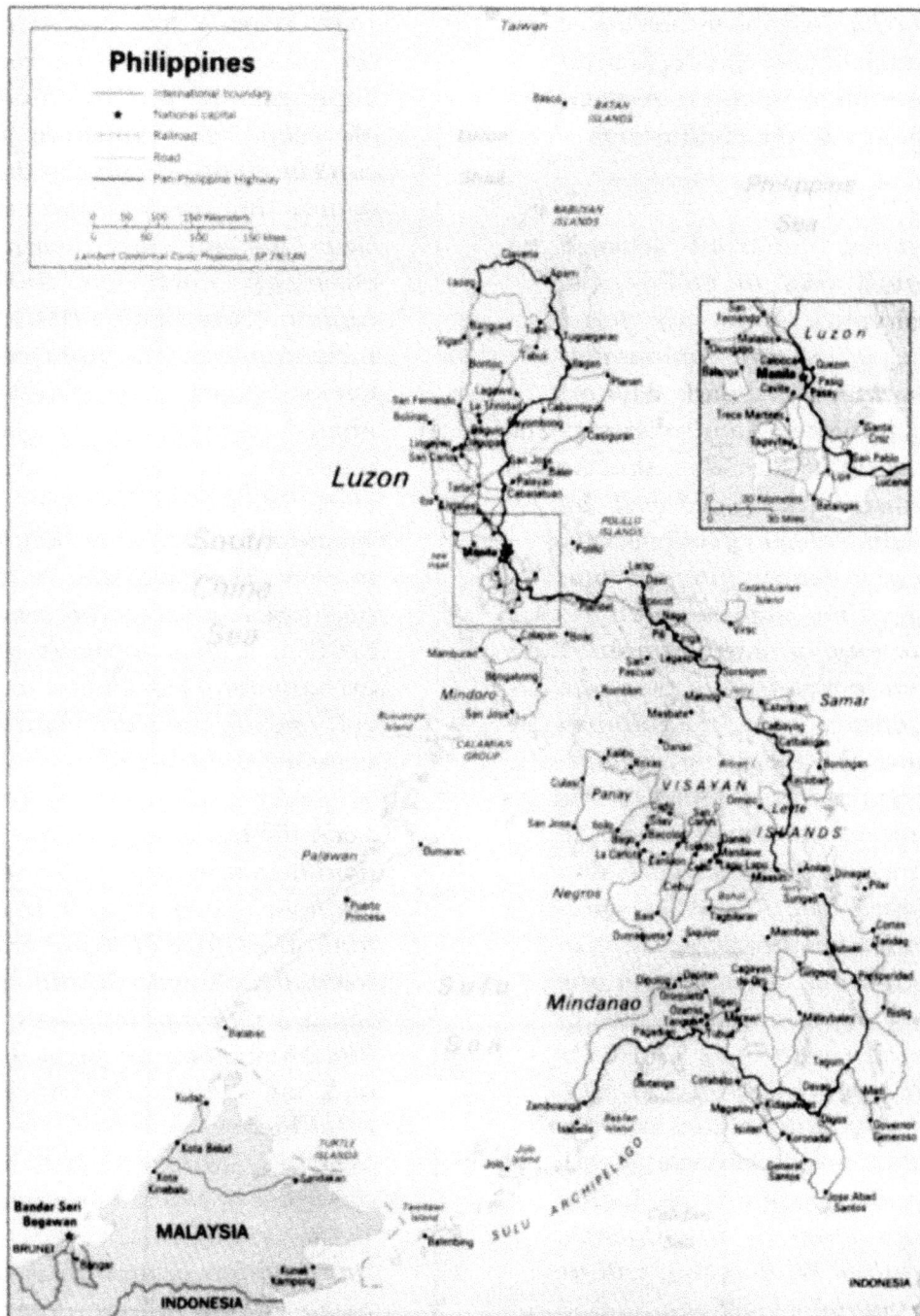

The Japanese attack on the Philippines in December 1941 was swift and effective.

the planes came in over a blind spot and their radar missed them. I had had enough of this. I went to Colonel Akin with facts and figures and explained the problem. Akin must have convinced air warning that we had something valuable to sell. The next morning, three air corps lieutenants reported to our station for liaison and plotting duties. Unfortunately, by this time, advanced warning by radio intelligence had lost most of its value. Many of our warnings were unheeded, and so many of our planes were destroyed while sitting on the ground. On 24 December, we were forced to move to Corregidor. Manila was declared an open city to prevent further damage to the civilian population.

Fabian: When MacArthur learned that our unit was in Melbourne, he got in touch with my boss, Admiral Leary. As the commander of the Southwest Pacific theater, MacArthur informed Admiral Leary, who was set up at Brisbane, that he wanted information produced by FRUMEL. Admiral Leary told me that we had to give MacArthur information but asked my suggestion on the best way to supply such material. I felt that certain restrictions were necessary to ensure security. Admiral Leary issued the following requirements: (1) Fabian or one of his unit's representatives will report to MacArthur's headquarters each day at 1400 hours. The FRUMEL representative will never be kept waiting in MacArthur's outer office. (2) No one will be authorized to make copies of any material provided by FRUMEL. (3) During the briefing of FRUMEL material, only MacArthur and his chief of staff, General Sutherland, will be present. Everyone else, including MacArthur's chief of intelligence, General Charles Willoughby, will be excluded from these briefings.

The military gave me a car. Every day at the prescribed time, I went up to general headquarters and talked directly with MacArthur. I briefed MacArthur and had the appropriate material with me if he wanted to read it himself. One of the most interesting briefings that I gave concerned the Japanese plans for Port Moresby in

1942. When I told MacArthur about the messages that we read about Japanese plans to invade Port Moresby, New Guinea, he said, 'that can't be right'. My idea of their strategy was that the Japanese would go to New Caledonia and then proceed to close off northeast Australia. I explained the whole COMINT process including how the information was derived from code groups. I convinced MacArthur to change his plans. A transport was scheduled to leave Townsville for New Caledonia the next day. Instead, they were sent to Port Moresby. The battle of the Coral Sea boosted the credibility of SIGINT. I was nervous about this exchange so I reported it to my admiral. Luckily we were right and there were no problems.

Even the higher-ups in the Navy had doubts about our information and methods of acquiring it. In the beginning, the Office of Naval Intelligence wanted nothing to do with us and certainly would not help with the funding. Then when we proved ourselves and had success, the Office of Naval Intelligence wanted control of COMINT. [Note: FRUMEL was under the Office of Naval Communications.]

Our intelligence was invaluable in the battle at Midway. This success silenced many doubters. FRUMEL played an important role. We intercepted the Japanese fourteen-part attack plan. We sent it to all the other units such as FRUPAC to get assistance with the solution. We beat our brains out solving codes, reading messages, and sending them in. When you saw the event happen, it was the *greatest satisfaction you could ever have.*

Whitlock: When compared to cryptanalysis, traffic analysis was a newer discipline. Commanders had doubts about cryptanalysis, but they were more suspicious of traffic analysis. The battle of Midway is a good example of the important relationship between these two disciplines. Traffic analysis provides the glue for the puzzle. A message by itself has no meaning; it must be placed in the proper context. Cryptanalysis gives the content of the message, but traffic analysis puts the message in the proper context.

Traffic analysts at FRUMEL identified the movement of ships toward the eastern Pacific. We reported this buildup and tabulated the ships that the Japanese were pulling together for this mission. Traffic analysts named every ship in the Japanese force except for one minor transport. Traffic analysts gathered all of this information before the cryptanalysts read anything about the impending attack.

An interesting question to me is, why did Commander Rochefort send out the fresh water message? [Note: The fresh water message stated that there was a shortage of fresh water on AF. The Japanese picked up this information and transmitted it to their units, confirming that AF was Midway.] Some people say that we could not identify where AF was so Rochefort wanted to trick the Japanese into revealing the meaning of the AF abbreviation. We knew AF stood for Midway. I believe that Rochefort sent

out the fresh water message to convince admirals such as Layton that intelligence derived from traffic analysis and cryptanalysis was correct.

Historians do not properly credit FRUMEL's role in the battle at Midway. Rufus Taylor, a cryptanalyst at FRUMEL, [recovered a single code group] that revealed the date of attack on 6 June 1942. He recognized the code group because he had seen [it] earlier in an unrelated supply message. He was able to deduce the meaning by comparing the [two messages]. Midway was a classic example of cryptanalysis and traffic analysis working together. More commanders trusted our work because we were right about Midway.

Managing Traffic Analysis with Akin at the Helm

After his escape from Corregidor in the spring of 1942, Colonel Howard W. Brown remained involved with intercept functions. Brown was part of the 126th Signal Radio Intelligence Company, which was the premier American radio intelligence company and had the most service in the theater. Frequently, he acted as a troubleshooter and problem-solver for Major General Spencer B. Akin, director of Central Bureau. Because of this role, Brown sometimes found himself in difficult situations. Brown was involved with Central Bureau from its beginnings in the bleak year of 1942. His experience illustrates the importance of good communication.

Brown returned to the U.S. in May 1945. After leaving the Army, Brown spent several years in the reserves and continued to work for McKay Radio in the Philippines.

After my arrival in Melbourne, Australia, I went to work as quickly as possible. My first duty station was at Townsville. There were twelve personnel operating this station; seven from the RAAF, one from the AMF [Australian Military Forces], and four Americans. The Americans who accompanied me were sergeants Carl Card, John Phelan, and Dick Nurse.

Managing traffic analysis is a tricky business. Monitoring enemy communications necessitates fast action. Our ability to issue warnings of air attacks as the Japanese concentrated on Port Moresby, New Guinea, was hampered by the slowness of communication [because of] distance. The challenge of getting intercept operators and equipment where they were needed was a daunting one.

In September 1942, I was summoned by General Akin, who told me to get a detachment to Port Moresby right away. As General Akin put it, 'The Japanese are thirty-five miles away and we need to move'. Later that afternoon, Wing Commander H. Roy Booth, the RAAF commander, who was also one of the assistant directors of Central Bureau, paid an unexpected visit to Townsville. He revoked my orders because they were not in compliance with predetermined policy. I tried to explain that war necessity [overrode] policy considerations, but Booth would have none of it. I thought General Akin had worked things out, but obviously he [had] not. I apprised General Akin of the situation. After a one-week delay, the detachment was on the job at Port Moresby. This mistake was unfortu-nate because it resulted in loss of lives.

Things ran more smoothly after this incident with Commander Booth. Americans became more involved in intercept. In October 1942, I took part in a conference at Brisbane where it was decided that we should have an intercept site close to Central Bureau. Americans ran this new station. We left Townsville, built the new station, and began work on 20 December 1942. We were located on a hill at Stafford, about six miles northwest of Brisbane. When the rest of the 126th (SRI) company reached us from the U.S. in March 1943, radio intelligence began to expand.

During my stint in Brisbane, I stayed as far away from Akin as possible. I enjoyed living out in the country with the troops. Whenever Akin needed something tough done in the combat zone, he would tell me to take care of it. When I returned, he never asked me if I accomplished my task. He knew that I got the job done, but he did not want to know how I did it. For example, in May 1943 I helped sneak a direction finding detachment into Port Moresby, New Guinea, to locate Japanese aircraft. Our equipment consisted of three SCR206 direction finders. In June 1943, when General Akin yelled for a direction finding net to root out enemy spotters at Dobuduru [northeast of Port Moresby], our detachment flew to the area to accomplish this mission. I selected the location for the expand-ed direction finding unit when the 126th moved from Dobuduru to Finschhafen [along the northern coast of New Guinea].

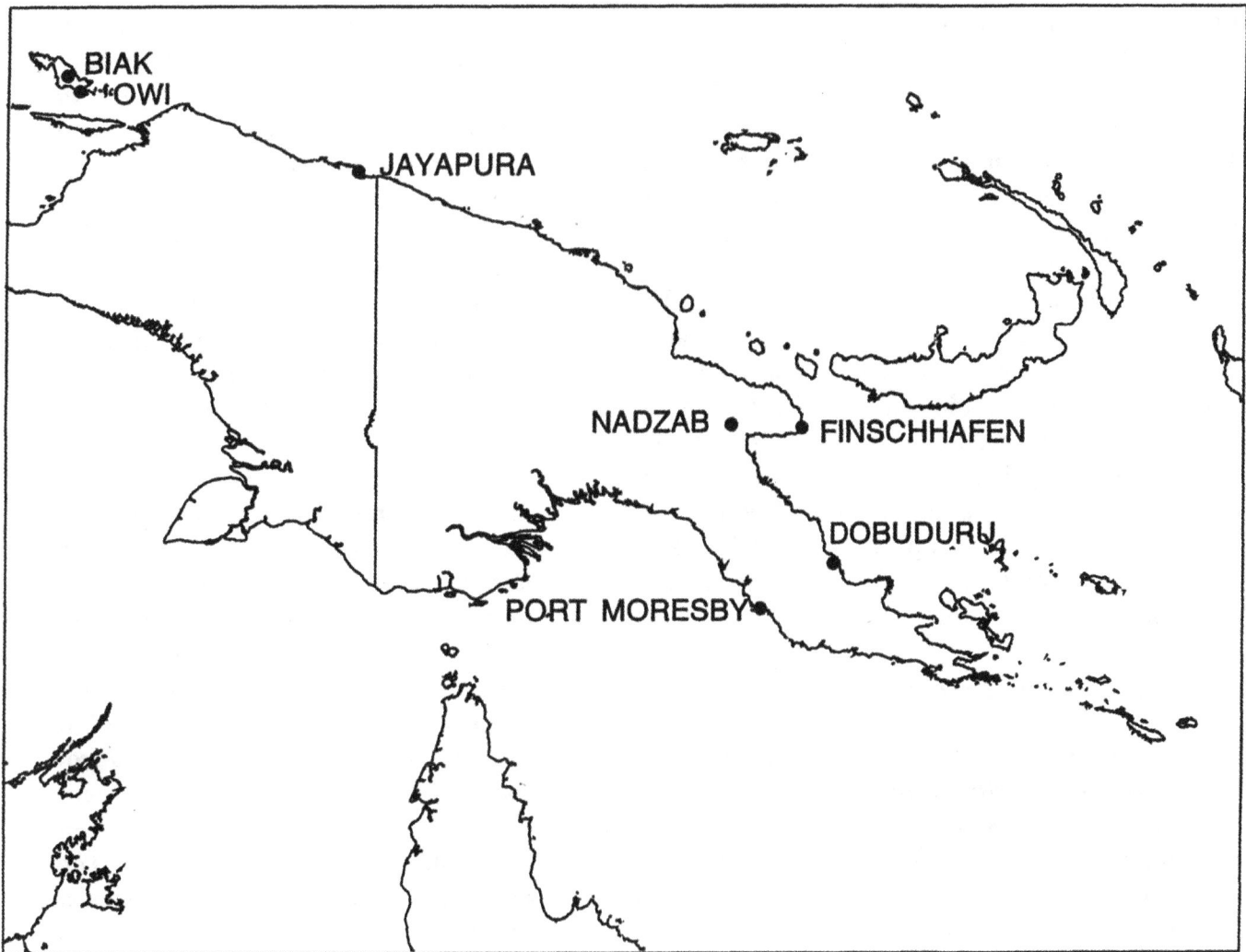

Intercept units kept pace with the Allies as they advanced through New Guinea.

Sometimes Akin had me solve problems at existing sites. Early in 1944, Akin told me to take over the terminal facilities at Darwin because of its poor performance. I found that the problem was really lack of equipment and poor training. I ordered more equipment and arranged for an instructor to train the personnel. Communication was restored in thirty days.

When MacArthur's headquarters moved from Brisbane, Australia, to Hollandia, New Guinea, in August 1944, the headquarters of the 126th SRI moved too. During the fall of 1944, Commander Booth selected me to be the commander of the forward echelon at Hollandia. I worked closely with SRI Clark, who was in charge of the intelligence section. My responsibilities included solving technical problems, obtaining equipment, and performing other administrative duties. In the winter of 1945, I returned to general headquarters and was part of Akin's staff. All in all, I had no trouble with Akin.

I Was the Meat in the Sandwich

The following recollections by Geoffrey Ballard were taken from his book *On Ultra Active Service*. They cover his experience as the Central Bureau representative at the advanced echelon at Port Moresby, Hollandia, and Leyte. The period covered is 1944 – the time when MacArthur made his greatest leap forward in the New Guinea campaign by invading Hollandia on 22 April. During the remainder of 1944, the war in the Pacific continued at a feverish pace culminating with the invasion of Leyte on 22 October, which was the start of the Philippines campaign. Ballard's experience and frustration with being the man in the middle demonstrate both the complexities of the logistics of fighting a war and the strains created in joint military command structures.

I left Brisbane for Port Moresby, New Guinea, in March 1944. I was the Central Bureau representative to general headquarters advanced echelon. My duties were to interpret the intelligence reports received from Central Bureau and its field sections in terms of operational significance, to stress both the limitations and possibilities of intelligence derived from traffic analysis, and to ensure the security of both the intelligence provided and its application in the field. Frequently I found myself implementing difficult orders from General Akin. For instance, General Akin was extremely concerned about the security of captured documents until they reached their destination at Central Bureau. General Akin demanded that all captured documents be in the custody of a single officer, transported on a four-engine plane, and preferably that the plane carry no passengers other than the officer holding the documents. I have vivid memories of arranging transportation of these documents. It
was ironic that a bundle of documents could rate the added security of a four-engine plane when so many human beings bumped over the Owen Stanley mountains and went on numerous other missions via that trusty workhorse, the Douglas twin-engine transport. I sure was relieved when General Akin himself decided to arrange for the transport of code books from the Yoshino Maru, which sank off the coast of Aitape.

I was in some precarious situations, either the man in the middle or the meat in the sandwich. General Akin issued orders on the spot, to me, a lowly captain. When I carried these orders out, my superiors at Central Bureau in Brisbane would counsel me about exceeding my authority. Toward the end of May 1944, General Akin officially informed me that general headquarters would move from Brisbane to Hollandia in August. The advanced echelon at Port Moresby would also move to Hollandia. I had the privilege of breaking this news to Central Bureau. They couldn't believe it. What would happen to the timely transmission of intelligence by Central Bureau in Brisbane when general headquarters was 3,000 kilometers away in Hollandia?

It was difficult for me to communicate the speed of the Allied advance to my colleagues back at Brisbane. They also had trouble understanding MacArthur's concept of general headquarters. According to MacArthur, a general headquarters belonged close to the battle front.

Moving the advanced echelon from Port Moresby to Hollandia was a messy affair. In Hollandia, life was very hectic. When a group of U.S. WACs arrived unexpectedly, I was told to immediately give them a one-day seminar on SIGINT. Another time, I had only one day's notice to fly to Nadzab, New Guinea, to give a two-week course on SIGINT to the intelligence staff at the U.S. Fifth Air Force general headquarters. The course proceeded smoothly until the mid-point. Then, the Fifth Air Force was told to move its general headquarters to Owi, an island just south of Biak. I assumed that this move would bring an end to my course. Not so. With the Americans, it was business as usual. I finished teaching the second half of the course on Owi, about 1,000 kilometers west of Nadzab.

The frenzy of activity increased as we planned for the Leyte invasion. We worked sixteen hours a day, seven days a week. Two weeks before D-day for Leyte, 20 October 1944, General Akin created another classic sandwich situation for me. Akin ordered me to get space on ships and enough equipment so that an RAAF intercept unit could take part in the assault phase of the invasion. The logistics people laughed at my request, explaining that all of the space was allocated long ago and that all of the assault ships were full. When I mentioned the urgency and importance of including the unit, the logistics people wanted to know why the unit was not on the original list of space allocations. The logistics people left me no choice. I had to pull rank by telling them that the chief signals officer wanted 6WU on this mission. Within one-half hour, space on the chief signals officer's communication ship

was allotted for the group. I received specific instructions about equipment loading, embarkation, etc. As General Akin instructed, the 6WU was part of the invasion. They distinguished themselves by alerting us that the enemy had spotted the approach of our convoy of invading ships. Shortly after the Leyte operation, Central Bureau told me that I had exceeded my authority: 'Planning remains a Central Bureau function'. This chain of command was more like a circle. I carry out the orders of the director of Central Bureau at Hollandia while the orders were criticized and virtually countermanded by the assistant directors 3,000 kilometers away at Brisbane. Naturally, I did not want to be offside with my own headquarters, but I was obliged to tell them that this situation could not be resolved their way. I had to follow Akin's orders. As a result of this exchange, tension developed between Central Bureau and its advanced echelon.

The tension between Central Bureau and its forward echelon was in no way reduced because, a few weeks after the Leyte operation, I had to deliver two other items. I had to tell Central Bureau that another RAAF unit was to be included in the Lingayen Gulf invasion, the next step in conquering the Philippines. The second item of information that I passed to Central Bureau was that general headquarters would be moving to Leyte in two weeks. With this move, Central Bureau would be 5,000 kilometers away from general headquarters. Central Bureau saw the necessity of moving to a more forward location.

When we moved to Leyte, we were called the forward echelon, to distinguish us from the advanced echelon, which was still at Hollandia. We immediately began planning for the Lingayen Gulf invasion. It sure was a relief to be replaced as the Central Bureau representative in December 1944 by Captain Neil Evans. All of the pressure and the sixteen-hour days were getting to me. I was exhausted. I returned to Brisbane and enjoyed doing administrative tasks for a few months. In July 1945, I became Central Bureau representative to the Southeast Asia command and finished out the war in India. I left the Army in January 1946.

Epilogue

The quiet heroes of the Southwest Pacific theater played a vital role in the Allied victory over Japan. The men and women who served at Central Bureau and at FRUMEL produced an astounding array of information about Japanese military operations. Their accomplishments were possible because of their dedication to duty, strong work ethic, fortitude, and attention to detail. Each participant recognized the importance of security and did not succumb to the appeal of fame or glory from public acclaim. They maintained the secrecy of their work throughout the war.

Breaking codes was a cumulative process that depended on the use of many disciplines. Cryptanalysts needed information from traffic analysis, and translators needed information from cryptanalysis. Teamwork was absolutely crucial to their mission. The solution to one military code frequently served as a lead in breaking the next code. In the Southwest Pacific theater, the pen was as mighty as the sword.

After the war, many of the men and women from Central Bureau and FRUMEL continued to serve their country. Some had distinguished military careers. Many others stayed in the communications intelligence field, and they all made valuable contributions as part of AFSA and NSA. The valuable lessons that these quiet heroes learned from their wartime experience led them to enhance U.S. security in later years.

Glossary of Abbreviations

1WU – One Wireless Unit

AAWS – Australian Army Wireless Section

AFSA– Armed Forces Security Agency

AIF – Australian Imperial Forces

AMF – Australian Military Forces

ASA – Army Security Agency

ATIS – Allied Translator's Interpreter's Service

AWAS – Australian Women's Auxiliary Service

CBB – Central Bureau Brisbane

CBI – China-Burma-India theater

COMINT – Communications intelligence

COMSEC – Communications security

FRUMEL – Fleet Radio Unit Melbourne

FRUPAC – Fleet Radio Unit Pacific

MOS – Military occupational specialty

NSA – National Security Agency

OCS – Officer Candidate School

OTRG – "On the Roof Gang"

RAAF – Royal Australian Air Force

RAAN – Royal Australian Auxiliary Navy

RAN – Royal Australian Navy

ROTC – Reserve Officer Training Corps

SIGINT – Signals intelligence

SIS – Signals Intelligence Service

SRI – Signal Radio Intelligence (Company)

SSA – Signals Security Agency

TICOM – Target Intelligence Committee

WAAAF – Women's Australian Auxiliary Air Force

WAAC – Women's Auxiliary Army Corps

WAC – Women's Army Corps

Sources

Chapter One

Oral History 05-83, Duane L. Whitlock; interviewer: Robert Farley.

SRH 045, Reminiscences of Howard W. Brown Oral History 22-82, Charles E. Girhard; interviewer: Robert Farley.

Chapter Two

Jack Bleakley, *The Eavesdroppers*, Australian Government Publishing Service, Australia, 1992. 8-10.

Geoffrey Ballard, *On ULTRA Active Service*, Spectrum Publications LTD, Australia, 1991. Chapter 23, "Preparing for the Invasion That Never Came." Chapter 25, "Spreading the Interception and Intelligence Net."

Oral History 56-94, Cecil C. Corry; interviewer: Robert Farley; follow-up interview with Charles Baker and Sharon Maneki.

Chapter Three

Oral History 22-82, Charles E. Girhard

Oral History 14-85, Joseph D. Richard; interviewer: Robert Farley.

Oral History 02-84 through 04-84, Abraham Sinkov; interviewers: Robert Farley and Samuel Snyder.

Abraham Sinkov interview with Dr. Ed Drea, February 1989.

Oral History 24-84, John J. Larkin; interviewer: Robert Farley.

Chapter Four

Oral History 51-94, Tristam B. Johnson and Donald E. Moreland; interviewers: Charles Baker and Sharon Maneki.

Oral History 02-85, Robert C. Christopher; interviewer: Robert Farley.

Oral History 30-84, Curtis H. Nelson; interviewer: Robert Farley.

Chapter Five

Jack Bleakley, *The Eavesdroppers*, Australian Government Publishing Service, 50.

Oral History 18-84, Sally Speer; interviewer: Robert Farley.

Oral History 33-83, Maryjane Ford Walter, Susan Cross Santa Maria, and Phyllis Purse; interviewer: Robert Farley.

Oral History 34-83, Victor Rose and John R. Thomas; interviewer: Robert Farley.

Chapter Six

Oral History 25-84, James B. Capron; interviewer: Robert Farley.

Oral History 21-83, David W.. Snyder; interviewer: Robert Farley.

Oral History 22-83, John H. Gelineau; interviewer: Robert Farley.

Oral History 32-86, Sidney A. Burnett; interviewer: Robert Farley.

Sid Burnett, "Japanese Intercept Down Under, Part II, Adelaide River," *NCVA Cryptolog*, Summer 1984.

Gordon I. Bower, "Potshot 1943," taken from "Japanese Intercept Down Under, Part II," *NCVA Cryptolog*, Summer 1984.

Oral History 15-84, John E.(Vince) Chamberlin; interviewer: Robert Farley.

Oral History 11-80, Robert D. Cahill; interviewer: Robert Farley.

Oral History 38-86, Ralph E. Cook; interviewer: Robert Farley.

Oral History 29-83, Joseph L. McConnel; interviewer: Robert Farley.

Oral History 30-86, Gil M. Richardson; interviewer: Robert Farley.

Chapter Seven

Oral History 09-83, Rudolph T. Fabian; interviewer: Robert Farley.

Oral History 04-83, E. S. L. Goodwin; interviewer: Robert Farley.

Oral History 02-79 through 94-79, Abraham Sinkov; interviewers: Robert Farley and Samuel Snyder.

Abraham Sinkov interview with Dr. Ed Drea, February 1989.

Chapter Eight

Oral History 05-83, Duane L. Whitlock; interviewer: Robert Farley.

SRH 045, Reminiscences of Howard W. Brown.

Oral History 09-83, Rudolph T. Fabian; interviewer: Robert Farley.

The History of COMINT 1936-1942, written in 1975, author unknown.

Geoffrey Ballard, *On ULTRA Active Service*, Chapter 28, "On Duty as Central Bureau Representative at Advanced Echelon GHQ, Port Moresby, Hollandia, and at Forward Echelon at Leyte."

www.ingramcontent.com/pod-product-compliance
Lightning Source LLC
Chambersburg PA
CBHW080520110426
42742CB00017B/3177